-- ABOU
DOCTORS an

". . . very readable, doesn't emotionally overwhelm, gives power to the family that thinks it is powerless."
S. H., LCSW -- Private Practice Therapist

"Assists the family out of denial. Gives concrete steps after diagnosis. Provides clear understanding and direction."
D. C., MSW -- Treatment Program Director

"Half the telephone calls I receive are from family members needing this information."
C. B. H., M.D. -- Treatment Center Physician

". . . fills the gap between AA, NA, and professional addiction treatment resources."
R. S. S., M.D. -- Treatment Center Physician

FAMILY MEMBERS SAY :
"For the person with no knowledge of alcoholism or drug addiction . . . everything you need to know to start an addict on the road to recovery."

"Easy to understand . . ."

"All the information you need to diagnose addiction."

"This book shows how one nonprofessional person can make all the difference in the life of an addict."

i

End Their Drinking? Drug Taking?
YOU DECIDE

**a black and white, no nonsense guide
for those who fear that someone is
drinking/drugging too much**

By Steve Gould

First Edition

Abyss Publishing, Knoxville, Tennessee

End Their Drinking? Drug Taking?
YOU DECIDE
a black and white, no nonsense guide for those who
fear that someone is drinking/drugging too much

By Steve Gould

Published by: **ABYSS PUBLISHING**
Mailstop 350
11831 Kingston Pike, Knoxville, TN 37922

Printed in the United States of America

Publishers Cataloging in Publication
(Prepared by Quality Books, Inc.)

Gould, Stephen C., 1933-
    End Their Drinking? Drug Taking? YOU DECIDE:
a black and white no nonsense guide for those who fear that someone is drinking/drugging too much / Steve Gould
        p. cm.
    Includes bibliographical references and index.
    ISBN 0-9637880-3-5

    1. Substance abuse--Treatment. 2. Alcoholics--Rehabilitation
3. Narcotics addicts--Rehabilitation   I. Title

HV5279.G68 1993   362.2'91'8
                                         QBI93-1122

Library of Congress Catalog Card Number 92-97523

DEDICATION

This work is dedicated to Clair Chamberlain Gould
July 30, 1911 -- July 3, 1961.

Clair Gould was a husband, a father, a good provider to his family and a friend to many. He was respected by his employers and peers. He taught me respect for the rights of others and if he knew any prejudices, he never displayed them. Clair Gould was a good man.

But Clair Gould was tormented. He was tormented by the disease of alcoholism and didn't know what the problem was. His family didn't know. To rid himself of this torment he tried formalized religion; it didn't cure the problem. He tried the Masonic Order, various vocations and geographical locations; they did not cure the problem. Finally he tried psychiatric medicine. The psychiatrist treated his problem with Valium and electroshock therapy; he committed suicide.

If this work is the instrument by which even one alcoholic or drug addict finds his or her way into recovery from the disease of addiction, my father's premature and unnecessary death will have served a purpose.

ACKNOWLEDGEMENTS

There are several people who must be singled out as essential to the beginning and completion of this work.

My life partner, best friend and wife, Marilyn, has made it possible for me to begin and complete the book. She has said again and again, "I want you to have the opportunity to write the book." Not once has she indicated that I should be doing something other than this work. She has supported me emotionally and us financially for more than a year. Marilyn has truly been my "rock," the support without which I do not function well. Without Marilyn, no book.

Benton Hodge is instrumental to the creation of this book because he was my mentor. Benton's gentleness, wisdom, experience and desire to serve mankind guided me through a profound personality change. Without that change, the person writing this book would not have existed and the book wouldn't have been written. In this sense, it is truly Benton's work.

As I thought about and talked about writing this book, it seemed to me there was a mine field of obstacles which could and would blow it away. Dick McCulloch would always say, "Just sit down and write. The difficulties you foresee will all be dealt with." Then one day he walked into my house with a computer and said, "Here, use it." After that I couldn't avoid starting the project which had been on my mind for six years.

Dick was an unwavering friend who has died since that day he delivered the computer. Because of the way he managed his life while enduring severe medical problems, Dick became an extraordinary role model for me. Dick, I thank you for your life.

THE EDITOR
Writing this book has given me a deep appreciation for the efforts of those who earn their living by writing. I was wrong in thinking that because I had lectured extensively on the subject I could easily convey the same message on paper. Knowing a subject, and writing about it in an easily understood manner, are entirely different. Good editing became an indispensable element of the message. Linda Driver magically appeared to do the work of editing at a time when I didn't even know I needed her. In addition to correcting hundreds of grammar and punctuation errors, Linda has contributed in large measure to the readability. Thanks, Linda.

Cover design by Kathy Barnes

STEPPING STONES

Each is given a bag of tools.
A shapeless mass and a book of rules;
And each must make; ere life is flown,
A stumbling block or a steppingstone.

R. L. Sharpe

The problem with stumbling blocks and steppingstones, is that we must first stumble over what we thought were steppingstones. It is only after the stumble that we can begin the creation of our true steppingstones.

We need not rage at the old stumbling blocks; they barked our shins and caused us pain for a reason. The pain of the barking was necessary for growth. Pain is the great teacher, motivator. Maybe the only teacher.

Steppingstones bring to mind visions of an adventure, a journey. The choice is ours. Begin the journey or continue to suffer. Pain is necessary; suffering is optional.

The journey of guiding someone into recovery from their addiction is beckoning, the steppingstones are laid out for you.

CONTENTS

NOTICE -- PLEASE READ

This book is designed to provide information about the subject matter covered. It is sold with the understanding that neither the author nor the publisher are engaged in rendering professional services. If professional services (legal, licensed, accredited, or certified) are wanted, these services should be sought from the appropriate source.

It is not the purpose or the intent of this text to publish all the information available on the subject covered here. You are encouraged to read other available material on addiction to mood altering substances so that you may utilize that information to suit your particular needs.

Every effort has been made to make this text informative and particularly useful to those who want the information contained herein. However, there may be mistakes, both typographical and in content. Therefore, this text should be used only as a general guide. The author and Abyss Publishing shall have neither liability nor responsibility to any person or entity with respect to any loss or damage caused, or alleged to be caused, directly or indirectly by the information contained in this book.

If you do not wish to be bound by the above, you may return this book to the publisher for a full refund.

CHAPTER ONE

THE PRISON OF ADDICTION

(A way to understand)

IF SOMEONE CLOSE TO YOU, A FAMILY MEMBER PERHAPS, DRINKS TOO MUCH, OR TAKES TOO MANY DRUGS, THIS BOOK IS FOR YOU.

To avoid using the clumsy wording of he/she, him/her, they/them throughout the book, the words "he," "him," "they" apply equally to women as well as men. Alcoholism/drug addiction doesn't distinguish between men and women, so this book won't either.

You are going to learn about the effects of alcohol and other drugs on ordinary people. You will soon learn whether the person you are concerned about is or is not an alcoholic/drug addict. You don't have to be a doctor, a psychologist or any other type of professional to be absolutely sure about this.

If the answer is "yes" -- he is an addict -- you will not want to believe it and you will hate that answer. But if you continue reading, *and take the action which is carefully outlined,* you will find support and hope for what can be done to bring serenity and peace of mind into your life.

The information presented here will teach you how to stop his drinking/drugging.

Four terms which appear often in the book are sometimes misunderstood or confused, one with the other. A brief description of each will help you understand the differences. The four terms are:
1) **alcohol** and other **drugs,**
2) **alcoholism** and **drug addiction,**
3) **alcoholics** and **drug addicts,** and
4) **you**

1) **Alcohol** (to be exact, beverage alcohol or ethyl alcohol) is inanimate. **Drugs** are inanimate. Alcohol and other drugs do not have a life of their own; by themselves they can't hurt anyone. Men and women have to use the alcohol or the other drugs before the disease can effect them.

2) **Alcoholism** is a disease. **Drug addiction** is a disease. Alcoholism and drug addiction are terms

12

which refer to the disease of chemical dependency. This disease will be referred to as "addiction" or "alcoholism/drug addiction" throughout the book.

3) Alcoholics are people. **Drug addicts** are people. These are ordinary men and women with the disease of chemical dependency or, as just stated, addiction. *Many people use alcohol or other drugs and* **do** *not become addicted.* **Addicts are people who use alcohol or other drugs and** *do* **become addicted, not because they want the disease, but because the disease exists.** People who suffer from the disease of chemical dependency will be called "addicts" or "alcoholic/drug addicts" throughout the book.

4) YOU are the instrument necessary to steer the addict you are concerned about into recovery, wholeness and good health; away from sickness and death. This calls you to engage in a process, to start a journey.

The purpose of this process, this journey, is to find a way to *stop* the addict you love from drinking and/or drugging and *start* him on the road to recovery from the disease.

THE PRISON
Addiction is a prison from which no one escapes alone; that is, no one escapes without help from

someone who cares about them. The reason for this absolute need for help will become clear to you after you understand the nature of the disease.

In the early stages of the disease, the prison has many large cells and the prisoner moves freely around within these cells. He doesn't even know that he is in prison. As the disease progresses the cells become smaller, movement within the cells becomes restricted. However, the prisoner doesn't know that this is happening. In time, the prisoner is confined to one small cell and still doesn't know that he is in a cell. At some point the walls of that cell begin to collapse inward, squeezing the life from the prisoner. He won't know, even at this late stage, the danger he is in. Eventually life is crushed from him. Just before death, he *may* understand how critical the situation is. But by then it will be too late.

Because man is a "family" animal, no one enters that prison alone. In the early stages of the disease even the non-addicted prisoners (the addict's family members) don't realize they are in prison. Soon, however, the non-addicted prisoners begin to realize that something is wrong; that their freedom has been restricted. At that point they will begin to tell the addicted prisoner that he is in prison but the door is open; it is time to walk out.

14

The addict not only can't understand the message, he will try to convince you (fellow prisoner) that you are wrong: it isn't a prison you are in, it is only life -- and a pretty good one at that -- that you are experiencing.

The choice is yours. You can remain in prison with your addict or you can start the journey out of prison for both of you. When I say "in prison" with him I am talking about *you* taking responsibility for *his* actions. Remaining in prison with your addict is known as "enabling." If you continue to enable, all of your disappointment, anger, frustration, and rage will continue. The lying, the cheating, the crying, the arguing, the pain will continue. It will be the same old story, over and over, nothing changing. The journey you **can** take is the journey to health, to peace of mind, to calmness in your life, to recovery from addiction.

If there is an alcoholic/drug addict in your life, reading this book, *and taking the action it recommends,* will change your life in wonderful ways. It cannot fail. However, there is hard work in taking the action. The process, the journey, takes time. Your time. Your effort. There are no instant cures. Serenity and peace of mind await you and the addict you are concerned about *if you are willing to do the work.*

15

If you decide that you do not want to do the work, you will remain in prison with him. It is your choice.

If you are going to help someone you must understand **why** they need help. All the information you need lies ahead. The chapter coming up will tell you whether or not there really is an addict in your life.

CHAPTER TWO

IS HE *REALLY* AN ALCOHOLIC?
A DRUG ADDICT?

(Here's where you find out!)

You can't identify an alcoholic/drug addict by sex, size, birthplace or age -- half a million of them are children under the age of twelve.

Nor can you tell by their blood count, liver size or shiny red nose.

But the way they behave always gives them away. Put together three or four telltale traits and you have an addict. Once you know that you are dealing with an addict, the direction of their life is as predictable as any well used path from the top of the mountain to the bottom.

To find out whether or not you have an addict in your life, you need to know how addicts behave. So, I will describe in several ways and in detail, what goes on

17

in the life of alcoholics and/or drug addicts. Here we go.

Ever feel as though someone has been reading your mail, as if a stranger somehow knows all about what goes on in your life?

As you read the following descriptions of addict behavior, you'll either begin to feel the answer is yes or, you will begin to feel as if that's not really happening in my life.

If the first case is true -- then you need to start the remarkable journey talked about in the previous chapter. You will do that with fear of the journey but also with the eagerness that says, "Finally, something positive can be done to end the craziness in my life."

If the second case is true for you and you don't identify with the description of the world of the alcoholic/drug addict, consider passing this book along to someone you think has a need for it. There are many people who are living with an addict who would thank you. That way you both benefit.

ADDICTIVE BEHAVIOR
The most obvious thing that happens in the household of the alcoholic/drug addict is, they get

drunk. I'm not talking about the once-a-year New Year's Eve or birthday party. I'm talking about frequent drunkenness.

Now, *frequent* has to be defined in whatever way describes your house or your business or your situation. Frequently may be once or twice or three times a week, or once or twice or three times a month, or once or twice or three times a year. In some advanced cases it may be daily. The disease of alcoholism/drug addiction isn't on any set schedule any more than any other disease. Just as no two people have the same number of spots when they have the measles, no two alcoholics/drug addicts "break out into a drunk" the same way or with the same frequency. However often it happens in your particular situation, you know in your heart of hearts that it is *too* often.

And *drunkenness* must be defined by the stage to which the disease has progressed. Drunkenness does not *necessarily* mean falling down drunk; vomiting drunk; fighting drunk; passed-out drunk; stealing drunk; driving drunk, can't go to work drunk. Drunkenness refers to the use of alcohol or some other mood altering drug to the extent that the person using it behaves differently-- in important and negative ways -- from the way they behave when they are not using it.

Right now you need to know that the overwhelming majority of alcoholics and other drug addicts are *not* living on the streets, homeless. Male or female, student or working adult, they are functioning in society at some level. That means that for the most part they are working or studying somewhere and coming home to the place they live on something of a regular schedule. They weave their drunkenness into the fabric of their daily lives.

Disorder and chaos rule the addict's household. Disorder and chaos can become so commonplace that you consider it to be a normal state of affairs. It is only when things get exceptionally wild and crazy that you realize that your surroundings aren't just like everyone else's. Then, soon after the wild and crazy episode has had some time to fade from your memory, hope springs to the front again and you think, "from now on it is going to be different around here." But, it never is.

The drinking and drugging may take place at home, at parties or at the local bar. The place makes no difference. The results are nearly always the same.

When you are forced to interact with him when he is drunk, or sick and hungover from being drunk, you feel as though you were dealing with a child under the age of five. Reasoning with him does no good at all.

Perfectly normal conversation with him seems to go in one ear and out the other.

It seems, at times, as if all you ever do is worry about his activities.

You are (sometimes) embarrassed by him socially because, under the influence of alcohol or other drugs, he acts the fool when other people are not being foolish.

He may prefer to drink/drug all alone, causing no trouble to anyone, he thinks.

Christmas, Thanksgiving or the family vacation have become a nightmare instead of the joyous occasions they were meant to be. You dread their arrival. Why? His drinking or drug taking escapades have nearly always screwed things up at holiday times. The turkey gets knocked onto the floor while being carved. The Christmas tree gets knocked over or there is a terrible fight about the right way to decorate it.

Most of us enjoy seeing a loved one mentioned in the local newspaper. We appreciate the distinction. But when that name is there because of an arrest for some offense related to drinking or drugging, like drunk driving or possession of marijuana, then we are terribly embarrassed.

When his name appears in the newspaper he explains away the whole thing by saying, "Well, I'm just like everyone else I know. Everyone drinks a little booze and smokes a little pot. So what's wrong with that? I'm no different than any one else, and besides, I can quit any time I want to quit. I work hard for what I earn to keep this place going. I deserve a little relaxation now and then. If I ever really get into trouble with this stuff, I'll quit, by God! I was just unlucky this time."

And then, days, weeks, or months later, when "It" happens again, you hear the exact same words from the exact same mouth and wonder, "Haven't I heard all this before? How can this still be going on? I was promised this wouldn't happen again and I believed; just as I have believed before. Surely I must be at fault here. This couldn't be happening if I hadn't somehow been part of the problem."

In the alcoholic/drug addicted household things get hidden, lied about, and covered up -- or the real meaning of things gets changed to something else. Examples:

Booze and drugs get hidden by the addict so he'll always have a supply. Money gets hidden by you so that he can't spend it on booze or drugs. When guests arrive and he is drunk, you hide him from the guests.

The boss gets lied to about why the addict cannot make it in to work some days. The kids get lied to about why they can't go on the vacation that was promised to them. The bill collector gets lied to about why the money is not available or when it will be available.

The parents aren't really speaking to each other and yet they pretend that all is okay when the kids are around because they must cover up their inability to solve the problem.

The kids' grades in school aren't anywhere near as good as they could be and the real reason for this isn't even known. Yet if the real reason were known, no one would talk about it because it is so important to uphold "the family image."

The grass doesn't get mowed and the yard doesn't get cared for as well as the rest of the neighborhood, and the reason is booze or pills, but no one is going to say that.

Learning how to remain sane with an alcoholic and/or drug addicted way of life draped around your neck is truly difficult. For instance: how do you react to finding that the family car has a deep dent and scrape all along the rear door and fender? And the person who was driving when the accident happened *swears* they didn't do it. And you believe that they believe, they didn't do it. But you also *know* they did do it. Then they end all discussion on the subject by angrily stating, "We're not going to talk about this any more. Period!"

**THE FOLLOWING CONVERSATIONS CAN
BE HEARD AROUND THE HOME OF AN
ALCOHOLIC/DRUG ADDICT:**

"Mom, why don't we ever go to McDonald's when we eat out?"

"Because McDonald's doesn't serve beer. Dad likes to have beer with his dinner."

"Dad, I can't bring friends home because Mom sometimes gets drunk and nasty in the afternoon."

"Grandma, why do Mommy and Daddy fight so much?"

"Grandma, why does Daddy get so mad when you ask him not to drink a beer?"

"Dad, I heard Grandma tell Aunt Mary that Mom was a drunk because she won't go anywhere without her pills. Is that why you won't let her drive, sometimes? Is that why the police took her to jail when she got into the fight at the grocery store? Mom said it wasn't her fault and she was sorry that it happened and it would never happen again in a million years. She said she was going to take us to the beach to have fun so we could forget about that and we don't have to go to that grocery store anymore. Won't it be fun at the beach, Dad?"

"Honey, have you let us run out of vodka? You know I've got this terrible cold. You know a couple of drinks makes me feel better. How in the world do you expect me to get any sleep without something to drink? Have you got any of your sleeping pills left?"

"Yes, I know I promised to come right home after work. Yes, I know I was supposed to start the charcoal early because Sally and Jim were coming for dinner. Look, I only stopped for one and the guys were shooting some pool and we got carried away, that's all. What's an extra drink or two anyway? It's not a big deal."

"Whadyamean, don't drink any thing else until after Sally and Jim are here? You know I can drink more than six other guys and still drive them home! Look, this is supposed to be a party; everyone has a couple just to loosen up before the party starts."

"I don't care if that doctor did say that my ulcer wouldn't get any better until I stopped drinking whiskey. I don't believe the drinking caused the ulcer. You know that my business depends on having a drink with the customers now and then. Besides, the whiskey relaxes me; that should be good for the ulcer, right?"

"Sure I smoke a little dope (marijuana) now and then. I also snort some coke, once in awhile. Why not? It doesn't hurt anything and everyone we run around with does it."

"I must be the most unlucky person in the world. Some people are really lucky. They don't ever get caught for driving drunk or smoking dope or drinking on the job."

"Sometimes I feel like my life is really all screwed up. No matter how hard I try I just can't seem to win. I don't know if it's because everyone's out to get me or I'm just no good.

TEENAGERS and YOUNGSTERS

If the person you're concerned about is a teenager or younger, the signs which should concern you are: unauthorized use of your credit cards, stolen money or missing household items; dramatic change in the clothes they wear; significant change in companions and activities; loss of interest in school activities or sudden loss of interest in personal hygiene; unexplainable failing or near failing school grades; open defiance of family norms; sudden disrespect for parents or authority; very noticeable mood swings; lying about activities and whereabouts; discovery of drug paraphernalia or the actual drugs hidden in the house or car.

YOU DECIDE

The descriptions, conversations and activities you have just read are not, and cannot, be *all* inclusive. Every situation has its variations, because no two people or households are exactly alike. The question is: *did you identify with several of the descriptions in a general way?*

If you felt as though someone had been "reading your mail" three, four, or more times -- *then alcoholism/drug addiction is causing problems in your life because someone you care about suffers from this terrible disease.*

You may be suffering from your own *denial* (see Chapter Four) and not want to admit that the problem exists. It is there.

Sometimes when something terrible is happening to us we feel all alone, as though no one else could possibly be experiencing this. Or, this is so destructive we must keep our secret inside the family, not let the neighbors know.

If you think you are completely alone and must handle this problem all by yourself -- nothing could be further from the truth. After you've read the next chapter you will understand that millions of people are dealing with this disease on a daily basis. Some of these people are doing a great job of putting their life in order, discovering peace and serenity -- most are not. **There is a way to include yourself in the first group.**

CHAPTER THREE

ADDICTS CAUSE PROBLEMS FOR MANY -- THE NUMBERS

(So you'll know you're not alone)

Most people have strong and *negative* feelings about the behavior of alcoholics and drug addicts. These feelings contribute to a "stigma," the disgrace, dishonor, and shame attached to being an alcoholic/drug addict.

Because of this stigma, family members (and others) keep secrets. You don't tell your neighbors that someone in your family has the disease of addiction. The result of not talking about the problem is that you don't know that others are feeling the same disgrace, shame, dishonor. While it is an absolute fact that you are not alone, it does feel that way because you keep the secret.

To help you feel less alone, less at sea in your struggle to aid an addict, look at some of the statistics about alcoholism/drug addiction.

IS *THIS* YOUR PROBLEM ?

AMERICANS SPEND $72,200,000,000 EACH YEAR ON ALCOHOLIC BEVERAGES.

Alcohol, a mood altering, addictive **drug**, is the main ingredient in alcoholic beverages. Beer, wine, and liquor (whiskey, gin, vodka, brandy, etc.) all contain some percentage of alcohol. The drinking of alcoholic beverages in the U.S. and most of the rest of the world, is legal and socially acceptable. Use of the drug alcohol has become so ingrained in society that those who do not use it are in the minority and sometimes even looked upon as strange. Knowing this, it is not surprising that a $72,200,000,000 industry in the U.S. is devoted to the manufacture, distribution and consumption of alcoholic beverages.

APPROXIMATELY 17,000,000 ALCOHOLICS LIVE IN THE U.S.

Something like 70 percent of the population of the U.S.(over the age of 15) drink alcoholic beverages. Of those who drink, one out of eight or 12.5 percent develop the disease of alcoholism. Multiplication tells the story: 70 percent, times 12.5 percent, times those over the age of 15 in the U.S. (population 254,000,000) equals 17,000,000 alcoholics.

30

MORE THAN 3,000,000 ADOLESCENTS
IN THE U.S. ARE ALCOHOLIC.
500,000 ARE UNDER THE AGE OF 12.

These numbers on adolescent alcoholics are supplied by the National Institute on Alcohol Abuse and Alcoholism, an agency funded by our federal government. It's scary to think of the science, the engineering, the humanitarian effort these kids will never perform unless someone does something to steer them into recovery from the disease of chemical dependency.

MILLIONS OF POUNDS OF
MARIJUANA ARE GROWN IN OR BROUGHT
INTO THE U.S. EACH YEAR.

HUNDREDS OF TONS OF
COCAINE ARE BROUGHT
INTO THE U.S. EACH YEAR.

THOUSANDS OF POUNDS
OF HEROIN ARE BROUGHT
INTO THE U.S. EACH YEAR.

Of the thousands of tons of illegal drugs manufactured in or imported into the U.S. each year, about 10 percent is discovered and confiscated by law enforcement agencies. If these agencies stop 10 percent, then 90 percent of these drugs become a product in the marketplace. There's an analogy here: many legal businesses lose or ruin 10 percent of what they produce. This loss is simply charged off as one of the costs of doing business. The illegal drug industry is no different. A 10 percent loss (to the law) is only one of the costs of being in business.

ACCORDING TO THE U.S. OFFICE
OF NATIONAL DRUG CONTROL POLICY,
AMERICANS SPENT
$40,400,000,000 ON ILLEGAL
DRUGS IN 1990.

Clearly there's a plentiful supply of drugs available to anyone who wants them. However, don't look to law enforcement agencies or your government at any level to solve your problem by stopping the supply of drugs. It can't be done.

One category of drug addiction is almost never addressed statistically, for a very good reason. This is the huge number of people who are addicted to drugs which are *legally prescribed to them by physicians*. It is nearly impossible to separate the addicts from the population which must use addictive drugs for legitimate medical reasons and does so responsibly.

SEVERAL BILLION TRANQUILIZERS,
AMPHETAMINES AND SEDATIVES
ARE LEGALLY PRESCRIBED
IN THE U.S. EACH YEAR.

We know that this "legal drug addict" population exists because of their death statistics. *There are more deaths each year due to overdose of prescription drugs, (usually in combination with alcohol) than there are from all the illegal drugs combined.*

MORE THAN 8,000,000 PEOPLE
ARE ADDICTED TO DRUGS IN THE
U.S. THIS DOES **NOT** INCLUDE
THE DRUG ALCOHOL.

A few years ago the National Institute for Drug Abuse, an agency funded by the federal government, estimated that there were 6,000,000 drug addicts in the U.S. Surely that estimation is too small. Within the past couple of years, agencies of the federal government have reported that roughly 18,000,000 people regularly use **marijuana**, a drug almost equivalent to alcohol in its addiction potential. Those same agencies have reported that 6,000,000 people use **cocaine** each month. Listen to this: cocaine is the most addictive substance known. Considering all the other drugs that people become addicted to -- narcotics, tranquilizers, amphetamines, antidepressants, sedative/hypnotics, psychedelics, inhalants, designer drugs -- 8,000,000 drug addicts in the U.S. has got to be a conservative estimate.

Adding the 17,000,000 people addicted to the sedative drug alcohol to the 8,000,000 people addicted to the various other addictive substances, you find that you live in a country which has 25,000,000 people suffering from the disease of chemical dependency. Many of your friends and neighbors are alcoholics and/or drug addicts. Think about it.

ONLY A SMALL PERCENTAGE OF
ALCOHOLICS/DRUG ADDICTS
RECOVER FROM THEIR DISEASE.

1% WILL BECOME INSANE.

3% TO 5% WILL SEEK
TREATMENT AND RECOVER.

95% WILL DIE PREMATURELY,
BECAUSE OF THEIR ADDICTION.

The really sad thing about these last four statements is: **it doesn't have to be that way.**

Drug addiction is a diagnosable and treatable disease which has a very high recovery rate when correctly treated by competent, trained professionals. The problem is **not** that addicts can't recover. The problem **is** not enough of them are being told -- *IN THE CORRECT WAY* -- that they need to recover. *THEY ARE NOT BEING TOLD THEY HAVE THE DISEASE OF ADDICTION AND MUST SEEK TREATMENT.*

EACH ALCOHOLIC/DRUG ADDICT
SERIOUSLY DAMAGES THE
LIVES OF AT LEAST FOUR AND PROBABLY
SEVEN OR EIGHT OTHER PEOPLE.

Since there are at least 25,000,000 addicts in this country and each one of them has a sickening impact on the lives of at least four other people, we are talking about a disease which affects the lives of almost half the population of the U.S. *YOU ARE NOT ALONE.* Millions of families are trying to deal with life on a daily basis with one or more addicts screwing things up all around them.

If you take into consideration the health problems, both physical and emotional; the financial burden from lost and destroyed productivity; the cost of law enforcement and keeping people in prison; the greatly increased cost of health and accident insurance; all because the disease of addiction exists: then you see a condition as big as or bigger than any other problem we have in the U.S. today. Without question, you are **NOT** alone.

Addiction is a disease rooted in ancient history. It is recorded that Cambyses, the King of Persia, some 550 years BC, was an alcoholic. In more recent times, Benjamin Rush, M.D., published a research paper titled, "Inquiry into the Effects of Ardent Spirits on the Human Body and Mind." The year was 1785. In this paper Dr. Rush talked about alcoholism being an "addiction" and a "disease." Modern research has proven that Dr. Rush, a signer of the *Declaration of Independence,* a surgeon and a General in the Continental Army, knew what he was talking about.

Several pages back, when I began laying out the statistics for you, (boring, I admit) I asked the question, "IS *THIS* YOUR PROBLEM?" I asked that question so I could give you this answer. The answer is a

loud, *loud,* *loud,*

NO!!

Your problem is not that alcohol and other drugs are so readily available.

Your problem is not that this disease has existed for thousands of years.

Your problem is not that millions of others suffer from it.

Your problem is only **ONE** person.

You only have to help one, not millions. You can be the instrument that guides one sick addict into treatment and recovery from the disease. And you don't have to do *that* by yourself. You're going to have excellent help.

Now, let's take a look at how this ordinary human being that you're concerned about progressed from being ordinary to having the disease of addiction.

Alcohol and Drug Use Stages

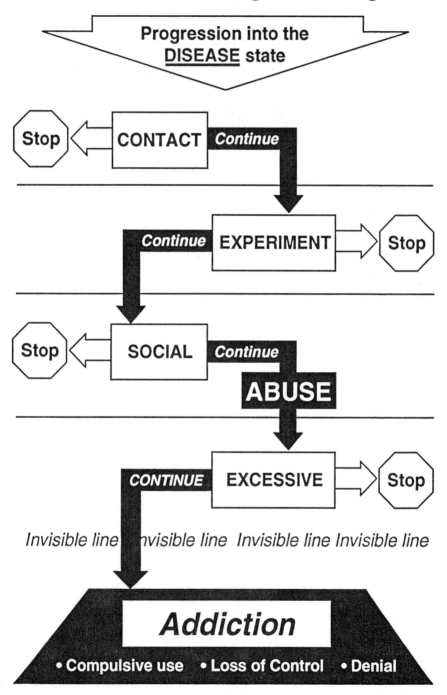

Progression into the **DISEASE** state

Stop ← CONTACT *Continue*

Continue → EXPERIMENT → Stop

Stop ← SOCIAL *Continue*

ABUSE

CONTINUE EXCESSIVE → Stop

Invisible line Invisible line Invisible line Invisible line

Addiction

• Compulsive use • Loss of Control • Denial

CHAPTER FOUR

HOW IN THE WORLD
DID HE CATCH THIS DISEASE ?

(Can this happen to almost anyone? Maybe)

On the page to your left there is a flow chart titled *Stages of Alcohol and Drug Use.* Notice the direction of the arrows. Starting with the word CONTACT, continuing through EXPERIMENT, SOCIAL, ABUSE, and EXCESSIVE, each of these way stations is accompanied by the word **stop.** After the arrow crosses the *invisible line,* there is no **stop.** This chart, with just a few words, lines and arrows paints a graphic picture of the path a person travels from being healthy to being cursed with the disease of chemical dependency.

I said earlier that addicts are ordinary people who have a disease which they did not want. Why can I say that about addicts? You and I both know, because it is common sense, no one *wants* to be, *asks to be*, a slave to alcohol or other drugs; forced to give up their honor,

39

money, self-worth, security and sometimes freedom to get the next drink or drug. Well then, if no one *wants* to become the person just described, it stands to reason that they don't deliberately *choose* to behave in ways that cause them to suffer terrible pain and remorse. Okay, if they don't *choose* to act that way, and those things happen to them *against* their will, why and how do they get to be an addict? *The answer is simple. They just go about their business in this world like anybody else.*

While reading through this chapter, occasionally look back to the chart called *Stages Of Alcohol And Drug Use.* As the significant turning points of the progression of the disease are described, the diagram will help you follow the flow from non-diseased to diseased.

At some point in our lives we **all** have that first time CONTACT with alcohol or other addictive drugs. This first contact usually happens sometime during the early teen years, though in some cases it may occur much later in life. It occurs because alcoholic beverages are served in the majority of homes in this country. They are also served in the deli's, the pizza places and all the top restaurants (as well as the not-so-top restaurants). Liquor stores, taverns, nightclubs and lounges are everywhere. Booze is sold in bait shops, supermarkets, convenience stores, drug stores, country clubs and gas stations. In addition, some state governments are in the drug peddling business with their A B C stores.

The people who sell beer, wine, and whiskey constantly tell us in their advertisements that using their brand of booze will make it lots more fun to go fishing, automobile racing, golfing, swimming, boating, card playing, dancing, volley-balling, marrying, lawn mowing, car washing, dining, graduating, etc., etc., etc. Their advertisements say to us, it's okay to be a little bit drunk.

And if you don't want to use the legal stuff (maybe you'd like the added thrill of being outside the law) then you have your choice of marijuana, cocaine, PCP, speed, LSD, heroin, glue, paint thinner, and all the prescription drugs being peddled in every neighborhood in the country.

There is a powerful message here for all of society: *use alcohol and other drugs. It's okay. They will make you happy.*

Even if you decide to stay completely sober by choosing to "Just Say No," the odds are that you will be exposed to some kind of addictive substance within the first 25 years of your life. Why? Because a doctor or dentist will legally prescribe a painkiller after surgery. When that surgery causes you lingering pain, you'll use the prescribed drug because you want to stop hurting.

It's true, the overwhelming majority of people do have a first contact with addictive substances.

At the point of first alcohol/drug use (contact) people are not addicted, not diseased. The power of free choice still belongs to them. They can make the decision to **stop** using the substance or, they can elect to continue using the substance in an EXPERIMENTAL way. Should they decide to continue experimental alcohol/drug use, they still have the power of choice because at that stage -- and here we have to be careful because there are exceptions -- they are not addicted. They truly can **stop** if they wish to do so.

If the casual experimenter decides to use alcohol or other drugs in a SOCIAL or recreational way, they might or might not keep the power of choice, the power to **stop**, for the rest of their life. **Example:** Remember a statement from the statistics; only one person out of eight who drinks alcohol becomes alcoholic. *The seven out of eight who do not become alcoholic are the ones who never lose that element of control from their lives.*

ADDICTION POTENTIAL

Let's pause at the SOCIAL point of the flow chart and take a look at addiction potential. We'll come back to the flow of progression in a minute or two.

Years of study by qualified people have verified the one-out-of-eight addiction potential for alcohol, but what is it for other drugs? At this point things get a little sticky because the subject is controversial. However, research and clinical observation do give us a general idea about the addiction potential of various drugs.

Picture in your mind's eye a scale, or ruler running diagonally across the page from the bottom left corner to the top right corner. Now picture a list of addictive drugs walking up the scale from bottom to top. The least addictive drugs will be at the bottom left, the most addictive at the top right. On the bottom left end will be marijuana and alcohol. While these are very dangerous drugs, not everyone who uses them will become addicted.

At the top end of the scale we find cocaine, the most addictive substance known. Specifically you will find "freebase cocaine" or "crack cocaine" which are the same thing but are obtained in different ways, chemically. Freebase/crack cocaine is heated and the

43

vapors are inhaled. The process is similar to the smoking of tobacco in a cigarette or a pipe. The drug passes through the lungs and into the brain in *ten seconds or less.* There are several ways of using cocaine but smoking it puts the highest concentration into the brain in the shortest period of time. Cocaine makes you feel good. Not just ordinary good but **really, really, *GOOD!*** If you have any emotional need (and what human does not) smoking cocaine satisfies that need perfectly and instantly. The sensation is chemically induced and false, of course, but nevertheless, the cocaine smoker feels euphoric, trouble free, without life problems. Difficulty does not exist. Many researchers now feel that *anyone who smokes cocaine will become addicted the first or second time they do it.* This is why cocaine is placed at the top of the addiction scale. Sniffing powdered cocaine up the nose (snorting it) is somewhat less addicting because the administered dose takes longer to reach the brain, the concentration at any given moment is not as great, and therefore the sensation of "perfectness" is not as high. There are people who have snorted cocaine and not become addicted. There may not be many of them, but they do exist.

Dropping down the scale a bit, we come to the opiate drugs. That is, drugs such as morphine, heroin, and opium, products of the poppy plant. While heroin and opium are not used by the medical profession, most of the rest of the drugs in this category are used medicinally. So, we know that not all users become addicted. However, these are highly addictive drugs. Using them for a long time will create addiction in most people.

Somewhere close to the top end of the scale lie the amphetamines. These are the drugs known as "uppers." They have brand names such as Dexedrine and Benzedrine. A very strong version is methamphetamine. A few years ago these drugs were widely prescribed to people who wanted to lose weight because they do take away hunger for awhile. But, the addiction potential is so great the medical profession has backed away from the use of these drugs for weight loss.

Right along in here, high on the scale, are the tranquilizers. Their names are Valium, Librium, Miltown, Xanax, Tranxene, Ativan, etc., etc. These are drugs which have a legitimate medical use but are also highly addictive.

Then we come to the sedative/hypnotics or sleeping pills. Dalmane, Phenobarbital, Secobarbital, Nembutal, Halcion are some of the names.

Then there are the analgesic pain killers Percodan, Darvon, Tylox, Aspirin with Codeine, Tylenol with Codeine, etc., and the muscle relaxants Soma, Maolate, Robomal, etc.

And finally we are back down on the scale to our alcohol/marijuana.

There are a number of other substances used by people to get "high," but they would just clutter up our scale. Do you get the idea that there are many reasons and many ways to "get high," avoid reality and become addicted -- diseased?

BACK TO THE FLOW CHART

Look again at the flow chart at the beginning of this chapter. (Page 38)

Those who are destined to progress on into addiction leave the level of SOCIAL use and begin to ABUSE themselves through the EXCESSIVE use of alcohol or other drugs; in this day and age, usually both.

Maybe the abuse of self through the excessive use of drugs is a temporary thing due to an extraordinary emotional condition. The death of a loved one, financial problems, or an extra amount of stress at work can cause such extraordinary conditions. If this is the case, when the condition comes to an end, the person who has been overdoing it will **stop** overdoing it and return to their old, sane pattern of use. They can do this because they are not addicted. They do not have the disease of chemical dependency. The return to the old, sane pattern of use should not take more than several days to a very few weeks at most.

Or, maybe the social user has some seriously bad effects from his use of drugs. Example: If a *social user* of alcohol or other drugs gets picked up for DUI/DWI and spends the night in jail, loses his drivers license for six months, pays a $500 fine, has his insurance canceled, and has his name published in the local newspaper -- telling the whole world that he is a drunk driver; he will not drink and drive again. Why? Because he has not lost the power of choice when it comes to the use of alcohol or other drugs. HE HAS RETAINED THE ABILITY TO LEARN THE LESSON FROM THE EXPERIENCE.

If, however, he continues, in spite of very negative consequences, to abuse himself through the excessive use of alcohol and or other drugs then he has lost the ability to learn the lesson from the experience and crossed the *invisible line* into the diseased state of alcoholism and/or drug addiction.

The line that is crossed into the diseased state of addiction is called *invisible* because no one can accurately predict who will become an addict; how much of which drug they will have to use; how long they will have to use it before the disease takes control of their life.

The disease of alcoholism/drug addiction is characterized by three things.
1. *COMPULSIVE USE*
2. *LOSS OF CONTROL*
3. *DENIAL*
Let's talk about those three things in detail.

COMPULSIVE USE

Compulsive use refers to the state of mind which *makes* the addict use alcohol or other drugs even when an ordinary person's common sense would tell them not to do it. Even when you think that he should *know* that he nearly always gets into trouble when he uses. Even when you think, "My God, that's crazy, why would anyone do that?"

Compulsive use has two parts: **1)** "Life is Supposed to Feel Good" and **2)** "Tragedy-Cause" amnesia.

The **"Life is Supposed to Feel Good"** part goes something like this: addicts and non-addicts are alike in that they want to do things that make them feel good and they also like recalling those things which made them feel good.

For **non**-addicts those things might be recalling a visit with a special loved one; enjoying a fishing trip shared with a pal; recalling the warm satisfaction of completing a difficult task at work; painting the house; recalling the glow of earned satisfaction from resolving a strained relationship; enjoying mowing the grass just right; etc., etc. There is no end to the list of things that can make people feel good. In thinking of things which make **non**-addicts feel good, you must understand that the activity which made you feel good required considerable effort and a sacrifice of time. As the old saying goes, "there ain't no free lunch." Every accomplishment has a cost. After the price (effort) has been paid, there is the warm glow of satisfaction from having performed well.

All of this wordy explanation is just to tell you that the formula is: *Effort followed by result followed by feel good -- effort followed by result followed by feel good -- effort followed by result followed by feel good.*

While it is true for the non-addicted person that "feel good" always follows "effort/result," it is different for the addict.

The brain chemistry of the addict is diseased. When he puts certain chemicals in his body all the *work* of "effort/result" is eliminated. With the introduction of certain chemicals the addict feels even better than the non-addict who **has** done all the work. The disease has short-circuited the process so that the addict gets the "feel good," the sense of accomplishment, from the use of the chemicals and none of the work is needed.

The more we feel good, the more we want to feel good, right? Why? It feels good! So where does this take us? Well, if you are an addict, it takes you to: **use more drugs because it makes you feel good!**

Now for the second part of COMPULSIVE USE, **"Tragedy-Cause"** amnesia.

The disease of addiction blocks the addict's ability to understand the connection between the pain he experiences and the drinking/drugging behavior which caused that pain. He can't understand that his actions caused the pain he feels.

If a non-addicted person has a very unpleasant experience, he learns the lesson from that experience and the lesson is: don't do that again. For instance: the very first time you smashed your thumb with a hammer or closed the car door on your finger, you made a firm and lasting decision to never do that again if there was any way to avoid doing it. You would, from now to the end of time, be careful with hammers and car doors. The reason you made that instant decision was pain. Great and excruciating pain.

Pain, both physical and emotional, **is the great teacher.** Maybe the only teacher.

Nearly everyone endures unpleasant lessons to avoid the pain of not learning the lessons. Math is an example. We learned basic math in school not because it was fun but because if we didn't learn it we would fail. Failing caused us pain at home. If even then we didn't learn some math, we suffered the additional pain of trying to get along in a world which demands that we at least know how to add and subtract. Sooner or later we learned enough math to stop the pain of not knowing. The pain of not knowing was the motivator, the teacher, that caused us to learn math.

ADDICTS AS WELL AS NON-ADDICTS LEARN FROM PAIN, WITH ONE EXCEPTION. THE EXCEPTION IS: ADDICTS ARE STRANGELY UNABLE TO LEARN THE LESSON FROM THE PAIN THEY SUFFER, WHEN THAT PAIN IS CAUSED BY SOMETHING THEY HAVE

DONE WHILE DRINKING AND/OR DRUGGING.

Please remember that statement. It is crucial to your attempt to guide an addict into recovery from his disease.

All people who have enough drugs in their system (of the type we are talking about here) will make bad decisions and behave in ways which are not in their best interest. This is true for non-addicts as well as addicts, because that is the nature of the action of drugs on the brain. The non-addict will, however, learn the lesson from the experience and not have to repeat it. Please think back to the non-addict who got picked up for driving while drunk. Anyone who drinks or takes drugs can make a mistake and get picked up for DUI/DWI *one time*. They learn the lesson and don't repeat it. Many addicts have many DUI/DWI's, all of which are extremely painful, both physically and emotionally. Why? **They have lost the ability to learn the lesson from the experience.** It is **not** because they are rotten, no-good, *x*x*x*x* who deserve to be hung.

Do addicts suffer pain from the bad decisions and rotten behavior that we see in them when they are drinking/drugging? Sure. Well then, we wonder, why don't they learn the lesson from the experience so that they won't have to experience the lesson again and again? The answer is that their disease creates "tragedy-cause" amnesia in them.

"Tragedy-cause" amnesia means they **CANNOT** tie their pain and suffering to the **CAUSE** of that pain and suffering -- which is contemptible behavior while under the influence of alcohol or other drugs. **After all, if they did tie the two together, they would have to quit using alcohol and/or other drugs, and using these chemicals has become their only means of feeling good.**

Okay, it is now time to bring "Life is Supposed to Feel Good" and "Tragedy-Cause" Amnesia back together to define COMPULSIVE USE. The addict thinks, and feels, and truly believes that the use of alcohol or other drugs does not have anything to do with any pain or suffering in his life. The **only** way he can feel good is through the use of drugs. So, the only thing that makes sense to him is to use mood altering chemicals. Because of "tragedy-cause" amnesia there is **no** reason not to use them. He is, in fact, COMPELLED to use drugs whenever he wants to feel good. And that's frequently.

LOSS OF CONTROL

The second characteristic of this disease is *loss of control*, which means exactly what it says.

When an alcoholic/drug addict begins using by drinking one alcoholic beverage or smoking one joint or popping one pill or snorting one line or shooting up just a little, he will very quickly lose control of two things: *how much he will use* and *what he will do while under the influence of the drugs.*

Loss of control does not happen 100 percent of the time. There are occasions when addicts **do** control their intake and behavior (at least during the early to middle stages of the disease). However, loss of control happens without warning and the addict can never predict when. Since they can **sometimes** control what they do, they feel as if they can **always** predict what they will do, and that's the problem. Their reasoning is, "If I don't intend to get into trouble, then I won't." After all, if it is true in your head, then it is true, right?

The truth is that loss of control is a problem caused by the disease; it has nothing to do with one's "willpower." The alcoholic/drug addict can't understand this -- is unable to understand this -- because the disease surrounds him. It controls.

LOSS OF CONTROL - - that was the easy one to describe and the easiest to understand. You have seen it with your own eyes. You know it exists.

DENIAL
Now comes the most difficult part of alcoholism/drug addiction to describe: *DENIAL.*

"Denial," according to *Webster's Dictionary*, means "refusal to admit the truth or reality." Well, sure. That was simple. That means I'm lying. NOT IF I AM AN ALCOHOLIC/DRUG ADDICT IT DOESN'T.

You see, for these folks DENIAL has an altogether different meaning. What it really means is that they can't tell the difference between the true and the false in their life when drinking and/or drug taking is involved.

When they are lying, and you know they are lying, *they* don't know that they are lying. In fact, they not only think they are telling the truth, they can't understand *at all* why you would doubt what they are saying.

Denial, for an addict, is a belief system. Remember: "if it's true in your head then it must be true." Reality does not come into play for an addict when their drinking or drug taking is the issue, because their denial system has become their reality.

Everyone has a denial system (also called an *ego protecting device).* Each of us makes mistakes daily and none of us owns up to all of them. We all like to feel good, which includes feeling good about the way we see ourselves. If we always owned and brought out every little imperfection about ourselves, or every little mistake we made, we'd soon destroy any good feelings we had about ourselves. We would end up with a lousy sense of self-worth. So, we gloss over these things with the "little white lie." Why? We like to feel good about ourselves.

There are very few people who don't want to feel good about themselves.

Anthony C. Greenwald has written, "The ego is a self-justifying historian which seeks only that information that agrees with it, rewrites history when it needs to, and does not even see the evidence that threatens it." And that's a **healthy** ego!

However, the person with a healthy ego can be persuaded to change his behavior when shown that a change in his behavior will serve him well.

Addicts can't be persuaded to change their behavior because denial has become so much a part of their life that it is, for them, the truth. Their reasoning is, "I don't have anything wrong with me. I only do the same things I see others doing. Therefore, there's no reason to change my drinking and/or drug taking behavior."

AN EXAMPLE
THE NON-ADDICTED DENIAL SYSTEM

Let's take a look at an example of the denial process for a healthy, non-addicted person and then compare it to the addict's denial system.

Picture a housewife who has been married for 18 years. She has a husband, three children, a dog, a cat and a four bedroom, three bath, 2,500-square-foot, two-story home to take care of. For the past 18 years she has cooked three meals a day and done the dishes, by hand, every day. She doesn't have an automatic dishwasher and most of the time her family is "too busy" to help out. That means she has washed dishes more than 19,000 times for this family.

One day she decides to stop washing dishes for four days just to get her hands out of the dishwater. Most would agree that this lady is entitled to four days away from the dishwater.

She will continue to cook so that her family can eat three meals a day. This lady understands that the dishes are going to pile up, along with the pots and pans. They will begin to smell after four days. The kitchen will begin to look more like a battlefield than the neat and tidy place we would expect. This is going to be an unholy mess and she's going to have to clean it up.

Because our housewife understands all the consequences of her decision, and is willing to accept responsibility for her actions, it's a sound and rational decision. It's not the decision that everyone might make, but for her, the benefits outweigh the cost.

Now we add some new information, an unexpected event which changes the consequences. Around noon on the fourth day, when the kitchen is at its worst and the smell is pretty bad, her mother-in-law shows up for a short visit without calling ahead to let our lady know that she is dropping by.

Now this mother-in-law is one of the world's best housekeepers and has never let the dishes pile up more than 30 minutes after the last meal. She's a real stickler about this sort of thing and is not above telling you and me her feelings on neatness and cleanliness.

Is our housewife going to tell her mother-in-law, "I've just decided to be a slob for awhile" ?

Of course she's not. No way! Her denial system will instantly come into play and she will say something like this: "The water is off in the kitchen because the framistan is broken. (What is a framistan? *No one* knows.) Bob tried to get one from the hardware store so he could fix the problem, but they're temporarily out. The new framistan is on order and should be in this afternoon. Bob will pick it up this evening, fix the water supply problem and I'll clean up this terrible mess tonight. Let's you and I go into the living room where we can talk away from all this mess."

This good and respected daughter-in-law has made up a little white lie which covers the situation beautifully. She is off the hook without a long, detailed, and possibly misunderstood explanation. *Her mother-in-law nods her head in complete understanding and sympathy.* **The unforseen consequence of her mother-in-law's disapproval, is instantly removed.** *The solution to the potential problem appeared out of our lady's mouth almost as if by magic.* She didn't think about it or plan it ahead of time. It was just there when she needed it. She is still a wonderful daughter-in-law because of the lie.

This little white lie is an example of denial from a person who is healthy. We all use this mechanism to protect the way we feel about ourselves and we use it frequently.

Take some time to think about your own use of denial. Haven't got any? What about your excuses for not getting things finished on time? What about that "don't-like-to-do-it" task at work? You didn't get the car washed as you planned? Oh, well, it's going to rain anyway. The *going to rain* is denial! That's your excuse for not washing the car. It makes you feel better about yourself when you have failed to live up to your own expectations. It's the little white lie that saves you from self-torment.

THE ADDICT'S DENIAL COMPARED
TO THAT OF THE NON-ADDICTED

Alcoholics/drug addicts are no different from other folks in that they also want to feel good about themselves. The further they progress in their disease, however, the more unacceptable their behavior becomes. They increasingly have to rely on denial to avoid self-torment. More and more the little white lie, the quickly devised excuse flows from their lips. Just as in our housewife's excuse about the water being off because the framistan was broken, there is no beforehand thinking about these things. The lie is not premeditated; it happens automatically.

Because the addict needs this ego-protecting device so often and in so many situations, it soon becomes a way of life. He's unable to tell the difference between true and false when it relates to his behavior while drinking and/or drugging. Denial is his reality, his way of life.

It's crucial for you to try to understand denial. You see, the addict truly believes that he is okay. Therefore, when you try to talk to him about his drinking/drugging behavior, what you say doesn't make any sense to him. He simply does not understand your reaction to his behavior. You are trying to get him to make a major change in the way in which he lives life and he can't see any need to change. Remember, by this stage of his disease, he *must* have alcohol or other drugs to feel good. He *must* live in denial because it explains away the unacceptable behavior caused by the use of alcohol and/or other drugs.

His thinking is: "I'm okay. There's nothing wrong here except that I'm sometimes very unlucky."

If you truly felt this way you wouldn't change either. If it ain't broke, don't fix it, right?

The difference between our housewife's denial and the addict's is this: if she were directly confronted about the dishes situation she might be a little embarrassed but she could and would easily explain her reasoning for allowing the dishes to go unwashed. She is accountable for the consequences of her actions. She would make some joke about it and go on about her business. *This lady would not repeat the behavior two weeks later and make up some other lie to cover her tracks because there wouldn't be any* **need** *to do this. She has no* **need** *to perpetuate the lie.*

Our housewife did not engage in socially unacceptable behavior.

Because addicts do engage in socially unacceptable behavior, and do repeat it frequently, they must live in denial. It would be emotionally devastating for them to accept responsibility, become accountable, for the consequences of their actions. They have a survival need to perpetuate the lie.

The socially unacceptable behavior seen in addicts is the result of the drug(s) in the system. Denial exists because they must have the drug(s).

SUMMARY

To put it all together, when someone has crossed the INVISIBLE LINE and begun displaying the characteristics of **COMPULSIVE USE - LOSS OF CONTROL - DENIAL** they are in the grip of the **DISEASE** of **ALCOHOLISM/DRUG ADDICTION.**

Diseases such as pneumonia, measles, ulcers, gonorrhea, rickets, scarlet fever (and hundreds of others) are curable; they can be completely eliminated from the body. Diseases such as diabetes and epilepsy and alcoholism/drug addiction are not curable but they are treatable. When properly treated, the negative effects of these diseases can be dramatically reduced.

But you must make no mistake about the disease of addiction. Once someone has it they will *always* have it.

Always having the disease is not all bad. Treatment for, and recovery from, the disease of addiction generally enriches and enhances the life of the addict to such an extent that he would not voluntarily return to social drinking and/or drug taking, even if he could do so without suffering all the terrible consequences of the disease.

WHAT DO WE KNOW ABOUT THE PROGRESSION OF THE DISEASE OF ADDICTION?

When ordinary people go about their daily business behaving the way ordinary people behave, they can acquire the disease of addiction. When this happens they are no longer ordinary people. They have become people who sometimes behave in socially unacceptable ways. That doesn't make them bad people, just sick people. The disease of chemical dependency (alcoholism/drug addiction) is no respecter of race, creed, color, sex, age or national origin.

Now let's look at several symptoms of the disease of addiction. Knowing some of the symptoms (addictive behavior) of addiction will help you to help the addict find sobriety.

The *DISEASE* of
Alcoholism and Drug Addiction

Symptoms

• Primary • Diagnosable • Treatable

- Lies about amount used
- Hides supply
- Blackouts
- Spends money on A/D, not on the kids
- Uses A/D to cure withdrawal
- Changes friends
- Misses work
- Depression
- Anxiety
- Fear

CHAPTER FIVE

THE SYMPTOMS -- DO ALL ADDICTS BEHAVE THIS WAY ?

(Well -- yes, most of them)

The chart on the page to the left lists several, but not all, of the behavioral symptoms of alcoholism/drug addiction. That's the subject of this chapter.

Because you and I have been around a great many people for quite a long time, we have learned what "average," or "normal," or "healthy" people do to get along in this world on a daily basis. There are no two people who act exactly alike, but the behavior of people in general is enough alike that we all know what is *okay* compared to what is *not* okay.

How do we know when someone, anyone, is sick? They act different. Their behavior is different from that which we normally see in them when they are not sick.

All illnesses have symptoms. Many (not all) of these symptoms are easily observed in a person's behavior; how they act when they are sick as compared to how they act when they are well. We all know when kids are sick by simply observing their behavior. They act sick because they feel bad. Their behavior is different from the way they act when they are feeling good. When kids are healthy they run and play and poke into things and laugh and cry and in general have a good time. When kids are sick they are whiny and angry and in general are difficult to be with.

The same behavior is true for our parents, brothers and sisters, spouses and friends. We can diagnose that someone is sick, has a disease, by just being around them. We sense that something is wrong by the way they act. In this sense, each of us is a diagnostician.

When a person has "gotten a cold," as we say, then that person will cough and sneeze, have a runny nose, feel stuffy-headed, have a headache, a sore throat, an upset stomach, maybe a fever, suffer from chills, and in general feel lousy. Do they have to tell us that they are feeling bad? No. We can diagnose that they are sick because when they have this cold they act differently than they act if they did not have it. They are displaying the *symptoms* of a cold.

Now, let's be very sure about what we are saying here. We are only diagnosing the fact that they are sick.

ALL OF THAT STUFF I'VE JUST SAID IS TO LET YOU KNOW THAT YOU *DO NOT* HAVE TO BE A PSYCHIATRIST OR ANY OTHER SORT OF DOCTOR TO BE ABLE TO DIAGNOSE THAT THE PERSON YOU ARE CONCERNED ABOUT IS SICK, TRULY HAS A DISEASE, AND DESPERATELY NEEDS HELP.

What if the person who we thought had a cold instead had something more serious such as the flu? Maybe it is pneumonia or tuberculosis or malaria. To find out *why* they are sick will surely take the services of a professional, someone trained and licensed in the science of medicine.

But at this point we don't care *why* they are sick because knowing why they are sick will not help us get them into recovery.

To guide this sick person through the healing process back into healthy living is also going to take the services of a person, or several persons, who know what they are doing. But at this point we do not need them. At this point all we are trying to do is confirm (maybe eliminate) your diagnosis that the person you are concerned about has the disease of addiction.

There are a great many technical, medically oriented symptoms for the disease of alcoholism/drug addiction. However, that is not what this book is all about. We want to be able to diagnose the disease of addiction through the use of socially observable symptoms. And we can do that because most of the people with the disease of addiction will act very much alike in socially unacceptable ways. Their behavior causes them to suffer pain and remorse and deeply bothers many people around them. And yet they do it again and again, even though it would be to their benefit and the benefit of others for them to stop behaving that way.

This chapter begins with a graphics page which lists many of the symptoms of alcoholism and drug addiction.

The words **PRIMARY, DIAGNOSABLE,** and **TREATABLE** are also prominently displayed on this page of highlights. They mean exactly what they say in reference to the disease.

1) A PRIMARY disease is one which exists by itself, is chronic and progressive. It is long-term and it always gets worse without treatment. Premature death is the

certain outcome unless something is done to interrupt the course of the disease (and even then, it can happen).

2) A DIAGNOSABLE disease means that we know what it is and what to look for in someone to determine if they have it.

3) A TREATABLE disease is one from which people can recover (or at least improve), if the right tools are provided and used correctly.

What follows is a description of some -- not all -- of the socially observable symptoms (behaviors) of the disease of alcoholism/drug addiction.

• ADDICTS LIE ABOUT THE AMOUNT THEY HAVE USED •

Yes, certainly addicts lie about how much they drank, or smoked or shot-up by exaggerating the amount. They will brag to their using friends how they were the one who, "had to drive everyone else home last night, and I drank more than they did." Why would they do this? DENIAL: it proclaims to the world, "Look at me, I can drink all this booze and still drive." "I am special because others look to me to take care of them." "That means I am alright." "I have no problem with drinking" (or drug taking of any sort).

To those in authority who question the frequency and amount of their drug use they will also lie, but in the opposite direction. The standard answer is, "I only drank a couple of beers" (smoked one joint -- snorted two lines --had one pill -- spent $40 or whatever is appropriate to the occasion).

The reason for this form of denial is that one, two, or three are small amounts and every one knows that a small amount of anything can't hurt you.

Notice the word "authority" in the paragraph above. Did you know that you are an authority figure? In the mind of an addict there are two kinds of people. There are those who drink and drug just about like they do and there are those who don't. Those who don't must be against them because they are not part of "the crowd." Parents, children, bosses, ministers, spouses, police, doctors, counselors, co-workers are all authority figures because they sometimes feel a need to question how much or how often an addict drinks or takes drugs.

Authority figures must always be led to believe that the addict is only using a small amount, and even that not too often, because if that is truly the case then obviously there is **no** loss of control. "If I'm always in control then what are you worried about?" "I'm not doing anything that others aren't doing." This is the message he **must** convey so that he doesn't have to look at or, God forbid, change his drinking/drugging pattern.

Don't let the expression "the crowd," used above, give you the wrong impression. It is not intended to mean only the motorcycle bunch or the street gang or the construction crew whooping it up after work. "The crowd" refers also to the physician who, all alone, is secretly injecting himself with Demerol and taking Dexamil. It refers to the U.S. Senator who is partying long after all the others have gone home. It is about the bank president and his golfing cronies. And it is about your 67 year-old-mother who is eating Darvon by the handful because she has convinced her doctor that she must have the stuff for her arthritis. She and her doctor make up "the crowd."

Notice that addicts walk both sides of the street. They either brag about how much or minimize how much they have used. That is the nature of denial and they do not see the sickness of their doing this. Quite a tightrope to walk, isn't it? Folks, let me tell you, being an addict is hard work.

• HIDING THE SUPPLY •

An addict will go to great lengths to have and keep a secret supply of the drug he likes best. This is not hiding drugs from the cops. This is hiding it to insure that he will have drugs to use whenever he wants or needs them. If no one knows about the secret supply then he can tap into it at his leisure. He thinks no one will know that he is using.

The list of hiding places is endless and runs the course from brilliant to stupid. A half-pint of whiskey floating in the toilet tank is rather common. More imaginative is the Valium tablets hidden in the "rabbit ears" antenna on top of the television set. All sorts of false containers are available for drugs of any description and are even available commercially. If you have two steam irons for ironing clothes then one of them can hold a supply of vodka and the family will never suspect it. Of course, when drunk, it is not always easy to remember which iron has the booze.

This symptom also includes the trick of making one thing appear as something else to conceal drug use. The addict who stops at McDonald's and buys a Coke, then pours half of it out on the ground so that he can then load it up with whiskey, is hiding the supply. He is attempting to say to all the world, "See, I am drinking a socially acceptable substance as I drive down the road." If while dining out at your favorite restaurant your wife says she has a headache, takes a couple of pills from her

74

purse and declares that they are aspirin when in fact they are something else, that is hiding the supply.

HIDING THE SUPPLY is a sure and certain symptom of addiction. You really don't need any other symptoms. Why? As they say in the courts, there is no socially redeeming value to the practice. If one's use of alcohol or any other drug is "social" or "recreational" only, then that use should be open for all to see -- socially acceptable. **Concealed use is recognition by the addict that what he is doing is NOT socially acceptable. If it were socially acceptable, he would not have to hide it.** While any of us may, on rare occasions, do some socially unacceptable things, addicts practice hiding the supply all the time.

• BLACKOUTS •

Temporary amnesia caused by the presence of a drug or drugs in the system is known as a BLACKOUT. This is not the same as passed out. Passed out is unconscious. People in blackouts carry on their activities just as if they were not under the influence of drugs **but do not remember doing it.** Painters paint houses; machinists machine parts; bankers make loans; doctors perform surgery; truck and auto drivers drive their vehicles etc., etc., while in blackouts. Not all addicts have blackouts. It is not necessary to have blackouts in order to qualify as an addict. Even a social user of a drug such as alcohol may experience a blackout. The difference between a social user's blackout and an addicted user's blackout is that the social user who experiences a blackout will learn the lesson from the experience. For instance, after a party where lots of drinks are consumed, a person who is not used to drinking so much may experience a blackout and not remember driving his car home and parking it in the middle of the front yard. Maybe there is an unexplained dent in the fender. The social drinker will be so terrified of not knowing what happened to him the night before and so fearful of what he might have done and can't remember, he will not drink and drive again. The alcoholic/drug addict who experiences blackouts has the same terror and fear but he is strangely incapable of learning the lesson from the experience. He has blackouts -- and drives -- all the time. He won't stop doing it.

• SPENDING MONEY ON ALCOHOL AND OR DRUGS INSTEAD OF PAYING THE BILLS •

This symptom is really self-explanatory. Any of us may be financially irresponsible for a bunch of reasons. The alcoholic/drug addict is financially irresponsible because he must have his drug to feel okay. That means that all other debts are secondary to any activity that helps him feel the way he needs to feel. He never plans to spend the "bill" money on his addiction, it just happens that way. Then he has to scrounge around and make do and borrow until next payday. Sound familiar? The kids are not deliberately neglected, it just turns out that way because the money gets spent before it ever gets to the house, in many cases.

• USING ALCOHOL OR OTHER DRUGS TO CURE WITHDRAWAL •

This symptom is also known as the "self medication" or "hair of the dog that bit you" cure. The idea is to get rid of the "hangover."

Hangover is an excellent term. It means "that which is left over from the night before." If you have ever had too much to drink at a party, that is, gotten high or drunk, then you know a "hangover" is really misery. Your head aches, your stomach is upset, your eyes are swollen and red, your skin is extra sensitive to touch, you feel anxious and nervous, your mouth and throat are dry and raw and you want to drink lots of water. But drinking water may make you sick to your stomach and cause vomiting. All in all, you would prefer that you hadn't drunk so much the night before and in the future you will remember the experience and not repeat it -- at least not frequently.

Non-addicts who suffer a hangover will take a couple of aspirin or Alka-Seltzer, drink some juice, eat a little food and be done with it in half a day.

Addicts, on the other hand, require more and more of the drug of their choice, just to feel normal, until they are continuously using so much that they get stoned or drunk every time they use. That means they will suffer the pain of withdrawal frequently. That pain becomes progressively more severe as the disease progresses and the body is less able to tolerate withdrawal because of physical deterioration. Even though the drugs are the cause of the physical deterioration the addict learns that the best way to get rid of a hangover, both physical and emotional, is to use some of the drug he used just a few hours before. This is the classic case of the vicious circle, ever continuing over and over, again and again.

If the drug of choice is not available, he will use whatever is available. For instance, if alcohol is the drug of choice then any of the other central nervous system depressants will do the job quite nicely. Many alcoholics have discovered that tranquilizers are a great substitute for booze early in the morning when they have to go to work. You can't smell those pills, you know. If he is severely sick then he may need to use something stronger such as Phenobarbital or Chloral Hydrate.

It doesn't take the alcoholic too long to discover that maybe those strong central nervous system depressants, on top of the central nervous system depressant alcohol, is too much of a good thing. After a while that combination makes one non-functioning. So the answer is to switch to "pep" pills. Amphetamines -- "uppers" as they are known on the street -- take care of the hangover and also give one the energy and false sense of self-worth to give the boss a good day's work. And that's important if you need to work to support your addiction. Now, however, within a short period of time he is forced to balance uppers with downers to be able to function daily. After a while no one can manage such a balancing act. When the addict *must* have amphetamines to function during the day (while still drinking booze, of course) and depressants to feel good at night as well as get some sleep, the end is approaching. This is the combination which brings about insanity or death. The only alternative is to enter into the process of recovery from the disease.

The addict whose drug of choice is in the stimulant category -- cocaine or amphetamines -- becomes extremely nervous and anxious from the use of and also the withdrawal from the drugs. Their nervousness and anxiety reach such a devastating state that they feel as if they are literally going to splinter into pieces. The only way to withdraw with some degree of comfort is to use a depressant. Much of the time this will be alcohol. As one can see, after awhile, the drugs just get all mixed together so that it becomes increasingly difficult for the addict to withdraw from drugs at all.

For people who have been using large amounts of certain drugs for a long period of time, withdrawal can be a medical emergency. This withdrawal can lead to death unless properly supervised by a physician who knows how to handle this particular medical problem.

Given the fact that addicts are very sick people physically, as well as mentally and emotionally, it is little wonder that one of the symptoms of the disease is that they use alcohol or other drugs to cure or stop the physical and emotional pain of withdrawal.

• CHANGING OF FRIENDS •

Alcoholics/drug addicts associate primarily, at least during their leisure time, with other people who over-use drugs. The reason for this is that if "everyone is doing it" then "it can't be wrong." The old saying that birds of a feather flock together is true. Think about it a little. Bowlers run around with other bowlers. The same is true of bridge players, musicians, golfers, mountain climbers, and all others of similar interests. One of the biggest reasons we enjoy associating with people of similar interests is that it reinforces our good feelings about ourselves. The unstated message is: "This is a wholesome activity because so many others are doing it."

If the person you are concerned about has gradually strayed away from old friends, and those friends were engaged in what most of society would consider healthy, wholesome activity, then there is a reason. If he now spends most of his time in the company of people who are generally considered to be very heavy users of alcohol or other drugs, then the reason is that he is addicted.

Another reason to run with the using crowd is that it knows where the drug suppliers are.

Maybe the one you are concerned about has just become a loner and runs with no one. He no longer spends time fishing, or gardening, or socializing. The symptom is the same. He has changed friends because of the addiction. Now his only friend is the drug.

• MISSING WORK •

Missing work refers to any scheduled activity. It can be employment, school, homework, housework, mowing the grass or visiting your aunt in the nursing home.

Alcoholics/drug addicts have a very difficult time keeping up with normal social obligations. Their need to drink or take drugs becomes their primary focus. They spend their time either thinking about it, doing it, or getting over the effects of doing it. All other activities simply stray into second place. This isn't a conscious decision on their part. It just happens as a result of the progression of the disease.

This is a good place to mention that the addict's employment is most, most important to him. There are two reasons for this: one, the job provides money to buy alcohol or other drugs and two, it provides a feeling of self-worth and self-esteem. The job declares to the world, "see, I am working therefore I can't be an alcoholic or drug addict."

When the addict's drinking and/or drugging interferes with his work to the point that the job is in jeopardy, you know that the disease has progressed a long way down the line towards the bottom of the barrel.

• DEPRESSION • ANXIETY • FEAR •

The person you are concerned about may be suffering from the emotional, psychological symptoms of depression or anxiety or fear or a combination of all three.

There are many, many reasons for depression, anxiety and fear to happen to and overwhelm people; non-addicts as well as addicts. However, if addiction is the cause of these things then the addiction must be treated first, or at least at the same time, for there to be recovery from depression, anxiety, and fear.

When the non-addict suffers from these serious problems he or she can seek help from the medical and/or psychological professional community. When they do so there is a great degree of probability that they will be helped and, in the normal course of events, will recover from these illnesses. *That statement is not true for the alcoholic/drug addict.*

Professionals who work at treating depression, anxiety, and fear (as well as all the other psychological problems common to man) almost never diagnose alcoholism and drug addiction in their patients because they aren't trained to see it when it is present. When they do diagnose correctly it is usually only after the addict is so far gone into the later stages of addiction that even the Village Blacksmith would make the correct diagnosis. Recovery is much more difficult to achieve at this very late time in the progression of the disease.

When psychiatric or psychology professionals do diagnose alcoholism/drug addiction in their depressed, anxious, fearful patients they generally attempt to provide treatment for the depression/anxiety/fear without first treating the addiction. Treating depression/anxiety/fear in an individual whose alcoholism/drug addiction is untreated is like shoveling sand against the tide: useless.

Depression, anxiety and fear which are caused by alcoholism/drug addiction will generally become of small importance, if not outright disappear, when the individual enters into treatment for the addiction and achieves complete abstinence from addictive drugs. If the symptoms of depression, anxiety and fear do not melt away when an individual stops using addictive drugs, these things can at least then be treated effectively without the causative and complicating factor of active addiction.

SUMMARY

Alcoholism/drug addiction is a primary, diagnosable and treatable disease -- with socially observable symptoms -- from which a great many people have already recovered.

The "cure" rate or success rate for treatment of addiction is very high. Of those who enter into the process of recovery some 75 percent eventually succeed in their efforts to stop using drugs, change the way in which they conduct their lives, and remain drug free. The tragedy is that so few are guided to the recovery process.

It is hoped that this small list and brief description of socially observable symptoms of chemical dependency will make it more comfortable for you to decide whether or not addiction is the disease which is screwing up the person you are concerned about. There are other observable symptoms. You can probably name a few from your own experience that aren't listed here. A person does **not** have to display all the symptoms listed here to be confirmed as an alcoholic/drug addict. A couple will do just fine.

—————————

There is an often repeated phrase in a popular Country/Western song which describes in a few words what the next chapter is all about. That phrase is: "Rolling downhill like a snowball headed for hell."

Your addict truly is a snowball bounding downhill, headed for a very hot place.

—————————

CHAPTER SIX

HEADED DOWNHILL LIKE A SNOWBALL HEADED FOR ....

(The trip to the bottom)

All diseases have a beginning, a middle, and an end. You and I don't die instantly from tuberculosis, pneumonia, cancer or addiction. Unless the addict suffers an early, drug-related, fatal accident, addiction can take years to develop into the full-blown late stage.

There are exceptions to this lengthy process, however. In today's world of easy access to a wide variety of drugs and society's permissive attitude toward multiple drug use, the trip to the bottom may not take as long as it did a few years ago. It can happen in a matter of months.

The chart on the next page summarizes the early part of your addict's trip down the road of addiction.

The Three Phases of Alcoholism/Drug Addiction

1 Early Phase **2** Crucial Phase **3** Chronic Phase

P R O G R E S S I V E

- Sneaks drinks . . . drugs

- Easily angered

- Drinks to cope

- Lies to cover up

- Avoids references to drinking behavior

- Increased tolerance

- Loss of control

Denial

THE EARLY PHASE

• SNEAKING DRINKS AND DRUGS •

Alcoholics/drug addicts most of the time look and act just like people who *do not* have the disease of addiction. But, when addicts are at a party where alcoholic beverages are being served, marijuana is being smoked, or cocaine is being snorted they will do whatever is necessary to get extra shares of the booze or drugs.

To do this, alcoholics may volunteer to bartend. This allows them to drink more without being noticed. If the party is in the living room but the booze is in the kitchen, alcoholics find reasons to stay in the kitchen.

Almost surely the addict, even at this early phase, will show up at the party having already been drinking or snorting a line or smoking some dope or taking pills. Normally there is no intention to be drunk or stoned when arriving at the party. He will have worked hard at the timing so that he has just the right amount of "buzz on" but doesn't appear drunk because it's important to appear normal. The problem is that if he doesn't get a head start he will be uncomfortable, ill-at-ease, at the party. He knows that a couple of doses of "something" will make him feel alright by the time he gets there.

89

And that's why he uses alcohol or other drugs in advance of the party.

• EASILY ANGERED •

Everyone experiences anger. It is a normal emotion and a normal reaction to certain situations.

Most alcoholics and a large percentage of other types of drug addicts are cursed with an anger which is swollen out of proportion to the cause. The anger you see in addicts is often vented or displayed in non-appropriate ways. This excess anger can often be present and observed early in the addict's life, prior to the drug usage.

The addict's anger is not "normal," in that it is triggered by events which do not ordinarily trigger massive anger in non-addicted people. For instance, most people would be only mildly irked if they dropped a can of beans while putting away the groceries. They might say, "Oh, damn," if they reacted at all. The non-addict certainly would not destroy something because of the dropped beans.

The alcoholic is different in that dropping the can of beans triggers a feeling of "I'm no good" to such a high degree that he can't stand the pain of the feeling. This feeling of failure is so instantly great that he must have relief from the feeling. Picking up the can of beans and throwing it through the kitchen window drains away the angry feeling.

Backing the car into an unseen post may trigger such violent feelings in an alcoholic that he will get out of the car and kick the door to drain away the feeling. The damage to the door can be far greater than the damage done by backing into the post.

The actions to relieve the feelings cause other problems. After throwing the beans through the window or kicking the car door to get instant relief from the feeling of "I'm no good," the addict then feels stupid for having done such foolish things. Then remorse and sadness set in. The best way to get rid of remorse and sadness is drinking or drugging, of course. Again, the vicious circle.

This kind of behavior baffles those around the addict. Even more importantly, the addict is at a complete loss to explain his actions. Of course, if questioned he will attempt some explanation but it won't hold water.

• DRINKING/DRUGGING TO COPE •
Living comes with a built-in set of problems for all of us. All people have worries, concerns, tribulations,

trials and "crosses to bear." The non-addicted person learns to deal with life problems in whatever way best suits him and his circumstances.

For the addict, the pressures of life can be avoided by drinking or drugging. He doesn't have worries, at least for a little while, when stoned.

Non-addicts can also experience temporary freedom from worry when stoned but they quickly learn that being stoned does not *solve* problems. So, they don't try to avoid life through the use of chemicals. Why is it that **addicts are strangely unable to learn this same lesson?** They have a **disease,** that's why!

Eventually the addict is deep into all sorts of life problems -- legal, job, financial, marital, social, emotional -- problems that have not been dealt with in any productive way. The stress of all this requires him to use alcohol or other drugs often. Staying stoned avoids the problems -- that avoiding problems by being stoned have caused.

Deep and layered trouble becomes more and more obvious as the disease progresses into the later phases but has its beginnings in the EARLY PHASE when the addict begins avoiding painful feelings by drinking to cope.

• LYING TO COVER UP •

Alcoholics/drug addicts spend a lot of time thinking about getting high, or actually getting high, or being sick and recovering from getting high. All this time spent "doing their thing" takes time away from far more productive activities such as mowing the grass, washing the car, going to work or picnicking with the family. This means that they are behaving irresponsibly and somewhere deep inside they know it. But, they can't not do it, so lying has to come into play. This lying is used to cover the irresponsible behavior that occurs when they are stoned or for the omission of productive activity when they are not stoned.

For a more detailed explanation of this process refer back to Chapter Four and the section on DENIAL.

• AVOIDING REFERENCES TO ALCOHOL/DRUG BEHAVIOR •

If you are concerned about the behavior of someone who is apparently destroying himself and all those about him with his drinking/drugging, then it is natural that you would want to see changes take place. You would try to talk to him about what you see happening to him.

But when you try to discuss drinking/drugging with him he gives short answers and changes the subject as quickly as possible. Why does he do this? The answer lies in who is doing the questioning. Remember the authority figures? If you are not part of the crowd of people who approve of his behavior, then it is important that he convince you that his behavior is okay. Your attempt to help will be heard by him as criticism. None of us likes to be criticized. Avoiding the discussion is a simple statement by him that there is nothing to discuss because there is no problem.

• INCREASED TOLERANCE TO ALCOHOL OR OTHER DRUGS •

As the months and years go by, the alcoholic/drug addict must use more alcohol and/or other drugs just to get the same feelings of "being okay" that he once got from a smaller amount.

The need for the greater quantity of drug is the result of the brain and other body organs building a tolerance to alcohol and/or other drugs. In the late stages of alcoholism, tolerance may reverse itself. Late stage alcoholics may get seriously messed up on small amounts of alcohol. The physiological reasons for both the increase and the decrease in tolerance are beyond the scope of this book.

• LOSS OF CONTROL •

Loss of control relating to the amount of drug consumed and the addict's behavior while under the influence was extensively discussed in Chapter Four. Please be aware that this is *not* late stage stuff. Loss of control occurs early in the progression of the disease.

At the beginning of this chapter, "THE THREE PHASES OF ALCOHOLISM/DRUG ADDICTION," a chart outlines the main points of the early phase. It is no accident that the word *progressive* is bold, outlined and placed within an arrow which points down! The following two sections of this chapter are headed with similar charts for the same reasons.

The Second Phase of Alcoholism/Drug Addiction

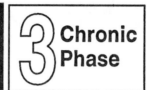

2 Crucial Phase

3 Chronic Phase

PROGRESSIVE

- Constant need to justify
- Often angry
- Guilt/remorse
- Extravagance/paranoia
- Changes A&D use patterns
- Job problems
- Marital problems
- Maintains constant supply
- Swears off (on the wagon)
- Physical and psychological problems
- Indefineable fears
- Loss of friends

THE CRUCIAL PHASE

This phase of the addictive spiral downward to death is described as "crucial" because the addict has demonstrated rotten behavior (while under the influence) for a long enough time that it is now recognized by most folks as being abnormal. It is the "crucial" time for someone to recognize the addict for the diseased person he is and take the steps necessary to guide him into recovery from the disease. The rotten behavior has gone on long enough to serve its purpose.

It is equally "crucial" in that at this phase of the progression the person suffering from the disease has the best chance of recovery from a psychological, a physical, and a medical standpoint.

Two factors make this the ideal time for the addict to begin recovering.

One: By now the alcoholic/drug addict will have suffered much pain from the many nasty consequences of his actions. **It is these consequences which must be skillfully used to get him involved in the recovery process.** Without the pain of these consequences, the addict would never enter into the recovery process because there would be no compelling reason to do so.

97

Two: At this intermediate phase the addict has enough physical and mental health remaining to be able to enter enthusiastically into the recovery process (after he has been forced into it). This makes the chances of recovery very good.

• CONSTANT NEED TO JUSTIFY •

At this phase of the development of the disease the alcoholic/drug addict's behavior is such that he is almost constantly in hot water with someone for some reason either directly or indirectly related to the use of alcohol or other drugs. That makes it critical that he create all sorts of stories to justify his actions.

This constant need to justify is an extension and magnification of the "Lies To Cover Up" previously talked about and is one of the many forms of denial.

• OFTEN ANGRY •

The inappropriate anger talked about in the "Early Phase" is now present much of the time and can be devastating. Spouse beatings. Child beatings. Abuse of animals. A fist or a foot through a wall or door. Destruction of property (such as golf clubs being broken after a lousy shot) is common. A building project can be destroyed, the destruction triggered by a minor mistake. This is insane rage which the addict cannot explain. It is more pronounced at this phase because he

98

is often out of control. Maybe this rage is anger at self. It sure looks that way.

• GUILT AND REMORSE •

The addict privately suffers enormous guilt and remorse as a consequence of his rotten actions. I say "privately suffers" because this is a part of his denial system. If he were to let anyone know that he was suffering from the things he did while he was drinking and/or drugging; then he would have to admit that he was drinking/drugging too much. And that might mean that he would have to admit he was addicted. And then he might have to do something about the drinking and/or drugging. Maybe quit.

In his mind, to quit would strip him of all sense of value, self-worth, self-esteem. This is truly unthinkable. So, he suffers guilt and remorse in silence, sharing the pain with no one who could help him.

The result of this guilt and remorse is, far too often, suicide. The number of alcoholics and drug addicts who commit suicide is a tragedy which can and should be prevented.

• EXTRAVAGANCE AND PARANOIA •

I've just said that addicts suffer guilt and remorse in silence because of denial. That doesn't mean that they don't try to make up for, and apologize for, some of the things they've done. Here is where extravagance enters the picture.

This is how it looks: Daddy has gotten drunk on payday, wrecked the car and blown the paycheck with the house payment due. How can he possibly make up for this? Easy. He goes to the bank and borrows money for the house payment **and,** more money to take the family to Disneyland. Now Daddy is a hero instead of a bad guy.

The problem here is that Daddy has done this (or variations of it) so often that his finances are in a mess and he can't really afford to do it. Being a hero instead of a chump has now placed him under extreme financial pressure, and because of his disease he doesn't know how to deal with this pressure in a healthy way. His solution for the stress is to drink or take drugs. And then it's off we go again, spiraling ever downward.

Paranoia is the serious mental illness which is characterized by feelings of persecution; that someone or something is out to get you, when in fact that isn't true. Alcoholics/drug addicts sometimes suffer from such feelings of paranoia without being truly psychotic. Some drugs such as cocaine and marijuana can be particularly bad about causing this.

There is the other side to this paranoia coin. Addicts who have been behaving irrationally or obnoxiously may actually have people who are "out to get them" in the sense that they are trying to get them to stop drugging, change their ways and shape up. The addict then correctly feels that "people are out to get me."

This messes up the addict's mind big time because now the worry is, "are they out to get me or is this just paranoia?"

There is a poster which illustrates this in a very descriptive way. It reads: **"Just because you're paranoid doesn't mean that they are NOT out to get you."**

Think about that poster just before you go to sleep tonight. If you felt that way you'd drink too!

• CHANGING THE ALCOHOL AND/OR DRUG USE PATTERN •

An addict changes or experiments with the booze he drinks or the drug(s) he uses and the way he uses them hoping to make it all work better. He wants to find a drug or way of using that will make him feel the way he needs to feel without all the problems.

Alcoholics are known for doing this. Switching from whiskey to wine or beer to stop stomach problems or heartburn is an example. Switching from whiskey to beer to prove that he is not an alcoholic is common. Mixing scotch with milk to sooth an ulcer has been tried often. Eating a large bowl of popcorn or a stick of butter before drinking, to prevent drunkenness, is an old trick tried by many. Switching from beer or whiskey to vodka so that others can't smell the booze, has been tried by almost every alcoholic. Mixing your vodka or gin or whatever with Pepto Bismol will prevent a hangover, right? (Sorry, that doesn't work.)

Drugs other than alcohol? Well, if sleeping pills are making you slur your speech and someone comments on it, then try switching to Tranxene or Xanax. Dilaudid make you vomit? Switch to Demerol. Or, add a little Dexedrine to spread out the effects of the depressant.

Change, change, change. Switch, switch, switch. Addicts will do anything to try to get rid of the bad results of their drinking/drugging. Anything except quit, quit, quit. (Actually they do quit, hundreds of times. The problem is that this compulsive disease won't let them *stay* off of booze/drugs for very long).

• JOB PROBLEMS •

The alcoholic/drug addict who has progressed to the crucial phase of addiction will almost certainly have experienced job problems. This includes professionals -- physicians, attorneys and college professors -- as well as truck drivers, machinists, factory workers, senior management people, politicians and homemakers.

An addict's job status may at first make a difference in what happens to him when his rotten behavior affects his job, but eventually the job will be gone. Workers who are paid by the hour and lower level management folks can probably build only a limited list of unexcused absences or drug-related accidents before being fired. Professionals and senior managers have a protective layer of co-workers who tend to defend or "enable" them, thus delaying the termination process. But in the end it's all the same. Unemployed is unemployed.

Many addicts develop an ability to sense when job problems are about to happen. They get good at leaving voluntarily before big trouble rears its head. That way they don't get fired. This allows them to get another job quickly without ever having to say that they have been fired. This in itself is a job problem. They float from place to place to place, always seeking "the right job for them," when the truth is that there isn't any right job for them until they begin the process of recovery from

103

addiction. This job hopping, and the geographical relocation which sometimes goes along with job hopping, is all a part of their denial system.

• MARITAL PROBLEMS •

If you will give a little thought to all that can have gone wrong in an addict's life by this stage of his addiction, and realize that much of what could go wrong has gone wrong, you will certainly understand why there are marital problems. The fact is, many, many alcoholics/addicts travel through more than one marriage. Multiple marriage and divorce is quite common among addicts for obvious reasons: a marriage based on and surrounded by alcoholism/drug addiction is truly "hell on earth."

Women are far more likely to remain in a marriage which is being destroyed by the disease of addiction than are men. However, this is not the place to attempt to detail the reasons for that phenomenon. The **real wonder** is that so many spouses choose to remain with their diseased mate, male or female.

• MAINTAINS A CONSTANT SUPPLY OF ALCOHOL/OTHER DRUGS •

The difference between *the sneaking of drinks and drugs* described in the EARLY PHASE, and *maintaining a constant supply* here in the CRUCIAL

PHASE, is primarily one of degree. By this stage of development of the disease the addict **must** be able to use alcohol or other drugs whenever the body demands because various body organs no longer function as well as they once did. Alcohol and/or other drugs have taken their toll. He could have serious medical problems if he suddenly stops drinking/drugging. He truly needs to go the "extra mile" to keep a supply on hand. A good description of some of the methods of hiding the supply was given in Chapter Five under the heading of "Symptoms."

In the final or CHRONIC PHASE of addiction he probably won't attempt to hide his supply of alcohol or other drugs at all. He just drinks/drugs openly because he doesn't have to keep up a false front anymore. Any sense of self-worth he once had is gone.

• SWEARING OFF •

"I'm going on the wagon," is a statement frequently heard from alcoholics. A slightly different version is "I'm riding on the water wagon," which means that he is only going to drink water, no booze. He is trying to convince you that he is quitting drinking, at least temporarily. Alcoholics/drug addicts often swear off drinking and drugging after a particularly bad binge that leaves them sick, shaking, and in trouble.

Have you noticed that people who are not addicted to alcohol/other drugs don't run around saying, "I'm going on the wagon" ? The truly social or "normal" user of alcohol/other drugs doesn't get terribly sick or into serious trouble. Social use of drugs means "without trouble," "without sickness"! The social user of alcohol or other drugs has no **need** to swear off or go on the wagon.

The addict's swearing-off period may last two hours, two days, two weeks, or two years. Swearing off doesn't cure the disease and at some point after stopping, he will start again because the disease will compel him to do so. Remember COMPULSION? If not, go back to Chapter Four and read it again.

Being able to stop for some temporary period of time is normal for addicts. THEIR PROBLEM IS NOT BEING ABLE TO **STAY** STOPPED. Because the disease is full blown at this phase, swearing off may happen frequently. When he starts to use alcohol or drugs again, LOSS OF CONTROL will raise its ugly head to prove that nothing has changed.

• PHYSICAL and PSYCHOLOGICAL PROBLEMS •

When the "snowball to hell" has rolled this far down the hill, the addict will be experiencing both physical and psychological problems. Alcohol is a particularly toxic chemical to pump into the body. There are some 350 different illnesses or problems which can happen to people from drinking too much alcohol.

Paranoia and depression have already been mentioned. Drug-induced psychosis (craziness) is common. "Flashbacks" or recurrences of psychotic episodes can occur from using certain drugs.

It is possible to *burn up the brain* with alcohol or other drugs. When this happens, there is no recovery from the disease.

The liver, which has to process all the drugs the addict puts into the body, can really get into trouble from drug damage. High blood pressure, ulcers, cancer, central nervous system damage, etc., etc. The list of possible and probable problems is long.

Stopping the progression before major physical and or psychological damage is done is vitally important.

• INDEFINABLE FEARS •
Fear is a wonderful human characteristic. It stops us from doing things which would injure or kill us. Without fear none of us would live long enough to have

to worry about the disease of addiction. That's healthy fear.

The alcoholic/drug addict suffers from another type of fear. It is fear that absolutely locks him up and makes him unable to function. This fear is indefinable, indescribable and totally debilitating. It is black, unknown, unknowable fear. It is fear with the power to turn the addict into a whimpering, curled-up ball. If you ask him what he is afraid of when this happens, he can't tell you. This is anxiety carried to its extreme.

The addict learns that a drink or drug will make the fear go away. Guess what he does about his fear?

• LOSS OF FRIENDS •
In Chapter Five, you learned about the *changing of friends* as a *symptom* of the disease which would eventually progress to the point that the addict has only other addicts as companions.

Loss of friends at this point means all friends, fellow addicts as well as non-addicts. The only friend left now is the drug.

When an addict's behavior has become so obnoxious that other addicts don't want him around or, he *prefers* to drink/drug all alone, the problem is truly severe.

NOW, THE SNOWBALL BEGINS TO MELT VERY QUICKLY.

The Third and Final Phase of Alcoholism/Drug Addiction

3 Chronic Phase

PROGRESSIVE

- Tremors and shakes
- Physical Deterioration
- Divorce
- Jail
- Value system breakdown
- Psychomotor breakdown
- Serious financial problems
- Loss of job
- Support system collapse

Death

THE CHRONIC PHASE

This should really be known as the "Oh my God it's probably too late" phase.

The addict can, and sometimes does, recover from this late stage of the disease but the difficulty of guiding him into recovery now is very great. Furthermore, there is the danger that he doesn't have enough brain function left to bring about a recovery.

To be very blunt about it, he may be beyond help at this point.

The hope is that you will be motivated to do something about him *before* he reaches this point.

• **TREMORS AND SHAKES:** All addicts suffer from "the shakes," when withdrawing from alcohol and certain other drugs.

But tremors and shakes at this phase of the disease refers to central nervous system damage. He will appear jittery or look as if he has palsy. The condition is visible with or without the drugs in the body but may be less visible when he is under the influence of drugs. Recovering from the disease and remaining free of alcohol and/or other drugs may or may not clear this up.

111

• **PHYSICAL DETERIORATION:** While it is true that the body will now have many things wrong with it because of the excessive use of alcohol or other drugs, most of these medical problems will not be visible. I'm talking about physical appearance.

Personal hygiene goes down the tubes. Dental care is long gone. He or she may often be unwashed, unshaven or without makeup. Going to the bathroom doesn't always happen at the right place. They simply cannot care about anything but the drug.

• **DIVORCE:** Of course there has been divorce; usually several marriages and divorces. The strange thing is that he is sometimes able to pull himself together long enough to find another mate, even at this late stage. After all, he needs someone to take care of him. Many times the new mate will also be an addict.

• **JAIL:** Having reached this stage of the disease, most alcoholics/addicts will have often been in jail for DUI/DWI or public drunkenness or "possession" or some other alcohol/drug-related offense.

Fact: do you know that roughly 80 percent of all the people in prison are there for an alcohol/drug-related offense or for committing some crime while under the influence of alcohol/drugs? The majority are addicts.

112

Being in prison is not treatment. They are not getting any better while in prison.

Going to jail is **not** a requirement for reaching this phase of the disease. One can be a late stage alcoholic/drug addict without ever kicking a cop in the shins. Little old ladies on legally prescribed pills do it all the time.

• **VALUE SYSTEM BREAKDOWN:** This simply means that the addict will do whatever is necessary to obtain the drug(s). Beg. Lie. Steal. Cheat. Prostitute themselves. Since they must have the drug(s) just to live, it no longer makes any difference to them how they get it.

• **PSYCHOMOTOR BREAKDOWN:** Have you ever heard the expression, "He can't walk and chew gum at the same time"? Well, that's what this is about.

Because of central nervous system damage, coordination is harmed. The brain tells the arms or legs to do something and it doesn't happen just right. During the days of Prohibition, this was known as "Jake Leg" from the damage caused by drinking Jamaican Rum. The person with "Jake Leg" will kick and flop his legs when he walks.

113

There are reasons other than excessive drug use for someone to develop psychomotor breakdown. *Not everyone who appears this way is an addict.*

• **SERIOUS FINANCIAL PROBLEMS:** Well certainly. If you owe everyone and pay no one, you have serious financial problems.

Folks, this is not wanton, rotten, shiftlessness or lack of willpower -- even though it may look that way. It is a matter of priorities. Alcoholism/drug addiction is a very expensive disease because alcohol and other drugs cost a lot of money. Nearly all the available money must go to buy alcohol or other drugs to insure survival. And at this stage there won't be much money because the ability to earn money has been lost.

• **LOSS OF JOB:** This is not just loss of **A** job, it's loss of **ALL** jobs. By this time the addict can't work much because he is really too sick to work. And his work history is so bad no one wants to hire him. He is not only unemployed, he is unemployable. His inability to work helps explain the "value system breakdown," and the "serious financial problems" as well.

• SUPPORT SYSTEM COLLAPSE •

Now we have reached the single most important **condition** which can happen to an alcoholic/drug addict, support system collapse.

Support system collapse means simply this: the addict's behavior has been bad enough for long enough. His obnoxious behavior has driven away all those who have been supporting him. He is alone.

It is now possible for him to begin recovery from his addiction because he has reached the CONDITION where all enablers (yes, you) have stopped bailing him out of the trouble he gets into. **Finally,** he is allowed to experience the full consequences, the full pain of his actions.

REMEMBER THE STATEMENT THAT PAIN IS THE GREATEST, MAYBE THE ONLY, TEACHER. WELL, SUPPORT SYSTEM COLLAPSE IS THE **CONDITION** *WHICH CAUSES SEVERE ENOUGH PAIN THAT THE ADDICT'S DENIAL CAN BE BROKEN. WITH THE DENIAL BROKEN, RECOVERY CAN BEGIN.*

DEATH

The word *DEATH* ends this discussion of the three phases of alcoholism/drug addiction for a very good reason. Death will come to the alcoholic/drug addict, *before his normally expected time to die,* unless something interferes with the disease process.

The addict's premature death can only be prevented by three other events. **1)** He ends up in prison. Because drugs are more costly and difficult to obtain in prison, he may be forced to slow down or stop using. If that is the case the disease will be temporarily on hold until he is released from prison. When he is out of prison and free to use alcohol and/or other drugs again, the disease will resume its natural, deadly course. **2)** He damages his brain so severely he has to be locked up in an asylum. There he will be cared for by attendants who will take care of him as if he were a vegetable, for the rest of his life. Surely he would be better off dead. **3)** He can enter treatment and recover from the disease.

To summarize the end results possible from the disease of addiction:
1) Premature death
2) Incarceration in prison

3) *Commitment to an asylum because of brain damage (or for some other severe medical problem).*
4) *Treatment and recovery from the disease*

WHAT HAVE YOU LEARNED SO FAR?

You know about the chemicals, the alcohol and other drugs that people use. You know that not everyone who uses chemicals becomes addicted. You know how ordinary people who never intended to become addicts travel from the first drink/drug into the diseased state of addiction. You know many of the socially observable symptoms of the disease of addiction. You know how alcoholics/drug addicts behave and about their denial. You know how the disease progresses from the mild early phase, through the severe crucial phase, into the chronic phase which all but destroys the addict's personality. You know that you are not alone; millions of addicts and those around them suffer from the ravages of addiction. You know what happens to addicts when the disease is allowed to run its course. You now know many things about the disease of addiction.

————————————

NOW LET'S LOOK AT WHAT IT TAKES TO
START ALCOHOLICS/DRUG ADDICTS ON THE
ROAD OF RECOVERY.

————————————

CHAPTER SEVEN

CREATED SUPPORT SYSTEM COLLAPSE -- THE SOLUTION !

**(Without this they get locked up
or die before they would ordinarily die)**

Now it is time to get truly serious about doing whatever it takes to get your addict to go to treatment, because treatment is the only way he can begin to recover from the disease of addiction.

The word "treatment" has been used a number of times to this point and yet it has not been defined. You would be justified in thinking, what **IS** treatment? The next chapter will fully explain.

Putting treatment aside for now, your *real* problem is to get your addict to go **somewhere** to get involved in **something** which will start the recovery process. At this point it doesn't make any difference what that somewhere/something is.

Please remember, the addict's thinking is that he **does not** have a problem and certainly **does not** see any reason to *go anywhere* or *do anything* to remedy something which **does not exist.** And if you were equally convinced that there was nothing wrong with you, you wouldn't do it either.

Since you know that your addict is not going to warm right up to the idea of quitting alcohol and/or other drugs, you need to plan a very determined, foolproof approach to getting him into treatment.

THE SUPPORT SYSTEM

Picture in your mind's eye a thick slice of onion. In the core of this onion slice, the very center, there is a single segment which is slender, frail and weak. Around this single segment there is a ring. Around this ring, another ring. Around that ring, another ring and on and on and on. Each of the rings is supporting the ring inside of it and is in turn supported by the ring which surrounds it. Without the surrounding rings the center segment, the core, cannot stand up. Its base is too small, its body too frail and weak. The center segment depends on the other rings of the onion for support, for life nourishment. If we peel and throw away all the surrounding rings of onion, the center segment will fall over for lack of support.

Each of us is much like that onion's center segment, its core. We all must have surrounding rings or elements in our lives to provide physical support and emotional nourishment. The surrounding rings or elements in the life of a human being are called: Mom and Dad; husband or wife; brother and sister; children; aunts and uncles; friends; co-workers; in-laws; employers; ministers; union stewards; doctors; lawyers, etc., -- *the support system.*

A *NATURALLY*-OCCURRING SUPPORT SYSTEM COLLAPSE

In the natural course of events, an addict's behavior becomes so socially unacceptable, so obnoxious that eventually all support -- from any source -- is withdrawn. This can happen within a matter of many months, if the case is terribly severe. It is more than likely going to take a number of years. Miserable years for everyone.

The addict will have borrowed so much money from family members and friends, without paying it back, that no one will loan him anything. He will have physically and emotionally abused his spouse(s) and children until neither will see or talk to him. His children will not allow him to visit his grandchildren. He will have promised and failed so often with brothers and sisters that he isn't welcome in their homes.

Lawyers and bondsmen pass the word that he is a lousy credit risk and they desert him. The family physician has long since given up. The family minister has talked until he is "blue in the face," and now won't go see him even though the plea is, "He is on death's bed." He has either killed the family pet or abused it to the point that even "man's best friend" runs away when he comes around. He is not only out of a job, he can't get one. His parents hate to see him come around because it always means trouble. And finally, he isn't welcome with the old drinking and drugging crowd.

ALL OF THE RINGS OF THE ONION HAVE FALLEN AWAY.

When all this has taken place and there is *no one* to help him; when his physical/emotional pain is severe; he has only two choices: 1) exist on skid row as a half human, begging for food, booze and drugs; 2) start the process of getting well.

Ninety percent, at least, of all alcoholics/drug addicts will have been killed by their disease **before** they reach a natural collapse of the support system. They will have died from addiction-caused cardiovascular disease or addiction-caused cancer or addiction-caused AIDS or addiction-caused suicide or addiction-caused liver/pancreas disease or addiction-caused uncontrollable bleeding, etc. Accidents -- auto, fire, falls, drowning, and so on -- kill the majority of addicts.

IF YOU THINK THIS WON'T HAPPEN TO THE PERSON YOU ARE CONCERNED ABOUT, YOU ARE WRONG. THIS IS A DISEASE WHICH HAS PREDICTABLE AND *CERTAIN* OUTCOMES UNLESS SOMETHING INTERFERES WITH THE PROGRESSION.

Of the small number of addicts who somehow manage to live until a natural support system collapse happens, three to five percent wander off to a half-human existence on skid row. Another three to five percent end up in treatment. Why? When the addict has destroyed his support system -- and his denial mechanism has no value anymore -- he surrenders to treatment. Maybe he begins to understand that alcohol/other drugs cannot provide wholeness, self-worth, self-esteem. Maybe something else will work. All is not dead; there is hope.

Isn't the solution to this whole mess obvious now? After the addict destroyed his support/denial system through years of obnoxious behavior, he entered treatment and began the recovery process. The solution is: don't put up with years of obnoxious

123

behavior, *create* **a support system collapse for him !**

A **Created Support System Collapse** is the condition, the place, we have been headed from the moment you opened this book. It is the tool you are going to use to force your addict into treatment.

THE *CREATED*
SUPPORT SYSTEM COLLAPSE

In the Created Support System Collapse the alcoholic/drug addict **is made to believe** that if he doesn't go to treatment to stop drinking/drugging -- **right now** -- then he is going to be left **totally** alone by **everyone** who could help him continue in his sickness. To say it another way, the support system collapse isn't going to happen slowly over the next several years, it is going to happen, WHAM - BANG - BOOM, all at once. Now. Today.

THE IDEA THAT HE IS LIKE OTHER PEOPLE MUST BE BRUTALLY STRIPPED FROM HIM. BLAMING OTHERS FOR HIS CONDITION MUST BE BRUTALLY STRIPPED FROM HIM. HE MUST BE CONVINCED BEYOND ANY SHADOW OF DOUBT THAT HE WILL BE LEFT TOTALLY ALONE, WITHOUT RESOURCES AND WITHOUT SUPPORT OF ANY KIND UNLESS HE ACCEPTS RESPONSIBILITY FOR HIS CONDITION AND ENTERS INTO A TREATMENT PROCESS.

When you read the word "brutally" printed above, read it as one of the kindest, most loving things you can do for him. If these things cannot be stripped from him, he cannot recover. The definition of brutal which fits here is: "unpleasantly accurate and incisive," as in "the brutal truth."

Bringing about the condition of support system collapse requires that a *team* of people work together to learn about the disease of addiction, then plan and carry out the action required to put your addict into treatment. The team's purpose is **not** to punish or seek revenge for past wrongs but to guide a suffering human being off his path of misery and death and onto a path of health, peace and happiness. This team will truly act with unconditional, non-judgmental love for the extremely sick addict. (If the team acts out of resentment or for reasons of punishment, the process will not work.)

This team needs to include all (or nearly all) the people who are important in the addict's life; all the people who have any opportunity to "get the addict's ox out of the ditch;" that is, enable him. (If I drive my ox into the ditch and you get it out for me, that is *you* taking responsibility for *my* actions. It is called "enabling.")

125

Since you've bothered to read this far it's obvious that you are vitally interested in an addict. Moreover, you are probably the one who is going to take charge of putting together the team which will **"condition"** the addict into treatment. Here's some good news for you. As I stated earlier, you **do not** do the work alone and *more importantly,* you **do not** take responsibility for the addict's recovery.

YOU ABSOLUTELY MUST LET GO OF YOUR ADDICT AT THE POINT HE ENTERS TREATMENT SO THAT HE CAN BECOME RESPONSIBLE FOR HIMSELF.

HE CANNOT DO THE WORK NECESSARY FOR HIS **SURVIVAL** IF YOU CONTINUE TO RUN THE SHOW.

If you coddle, pamper, excuse, pardon, indulge, take care of, make decisions for, -- in a word, ENABLE him after he has gone to treatment -- you will be sabotaging the treatment.

Your understanding about what to do **after** he has gone to treatment is as important as your need to understand what it takes to get him into treatment. Simply put, you must now let him do the work. If you try to do it for him, he is going to die. The last chapter of this book addresses the things *you need to do* after he has gone to treatment.

PUTTING THE TEAM TOGETHER

Think about the addicts "onion." Who are the people who make up the rings around him: wife or husband, children, parents, brothers and sisters, aunts and uncles, friends (non-addicted), in-laws, boss, etc. These are the people who have, for a very long time, "gotten his ox out of the ditch." Write their names down because you will need a checklist of these people. You are going to ask them individually for a commitment of time and effort and emotional upheaval to bring about a significant and positive change in the life of someone they care about.

My recommendation to you is that you first meet with each of these people on a personal, one-on-one basis. Use the telephone *only* to make appointments with the person you want to see. You do it this way because you are going to have to be very persuasive to get all the people you need to help you do this job; and that is easier done in person. It is an old sales truism that it is much more difficult to say no, face to face, than to say no on the telephone.

The best way for you to get all the people you will need for this effort is to work step by step, allowing them to back out if they are uncomfortable. Don't ask for total commitment in the very beginning. Most folks will be eager to help you accomplish your goal and go all the way with you **IF** they understand the process and what is at stake. But they, like you, have to unlearn some old ideas before the new ideas you're learning here can be believed and put to work. This takes time and persuasion.

For starters, you can explain that you are deeply concerned about "Xxxxxx" because you are convinced that he has a disease which is killing him, and that you are trying to find a way to guide him back to health. Don't try to explain "support system collapse" on the telephone. All you need to say is that you'd like a personal meeting because you need their help, and want to talk about the problem.

As you meet with each of the potential team members you explain your reasons for knowing that "Xxxxxx" is an addict. Then you can tell them why it is so vital that **many** people get involved to help "Xxxxxx" find a way into the recovery process. Also at these individual meetings you ask the potential team members to agree to two other small things: 1) another meeting with all the people who might be able to help so that there can be a group discussion about the problem and; 2) a firm promise from them that they will **not** discuss any of this with "Xxxxxx" even if they are not in agreement with you at this time.

This last point is very important. You don't want your efforts sabotaged before everyone who will be involved has a chance to discuss the entire process. There will be more about sabotage later. It can rear its ugly head at any time from now until the process is complete.

ENLISTING PROFESSIONAL HELP

The Created Support System Collapse you are about to conduct will not work if it is attempted in any sort of willy-nilly or less-than-professional manner. This process is going to require very careful planning, training and cooperation among the team members. Knowing that you are being guided by a trained, experienced professional will make the goal of putting your addict into treatment much more comfortable.

The following statement is not meant as any sort of "put down" to you but only as a statement of fact. *If you knew how to do the work necessary to guide your addict into recovery -- without a professional to help you -- you would have already done it.* You should eagerly seek a professional counselor for this work.

You can find a *counselor* who has been trained in teaching and conducting "support system collapse" by contacting one of your local alcoholism/drug addiction treatment centers. These centers can be found listed in the Yellow Pages of the telephone book.

If you live in a large community there will be many listings under the heading ALCOHOLISM. Even if you live in a very small community there will be some listings of centers located within reasonable driving distance.

Not all centers have counselors who do this work. Some who do this work do it better than others. (This is not a belittling statement. Some machinists are better than others. Some painters are better than others etc., etc.) It is very important that you be comfortable with the counselor who will be guiding you. You will need great confidence in this person's ability to help you get the job done right. Make appointments with several of these counselors. Then sit down with each of them to talk about your particular situation.

Some centers/counselors charge for this service, some do not. After you learn how much work this person does for you and how important they are to the success of the project, a reasonable fee will seem like no big deal.

After you have discussed your situation with several counselors, you are then ready to make an informed decision about the person you want to trust with this vitally important job.

THE WORD "INTERVENTION"

What should you say when you call an alcoholism/drug addiction treatment center asking for help? Well, now I must introduce a word that I have intentionally avoided using until this very moment. That word is *INTERVENTION.*

The process that I've described to you as a **Created Support System Collapse** is called *"intervention"* by most treatment center employees. Because of this, when you call a treatment center you should ask them if they teach *and* conduct "interventions." If they say they do, make an appointment to discuss your situation with them in person.

There are a number of fine books and many articles on the subject of "intervention," many of which include the word "intervention" in the title. One, by Dr. Vernon E. Johnson, who pioneered this process, is titled, *Intervention.* I recommend that you read it.

I have purposely not used the word "intervention" to this point, and will avoid using it through the rest of this book because of the possibility of misunderstanding by many people. "Intervention" is a noun which has so frequently been used as a verb by people who work in the field of addiction treatment that the verb-for-noun usage is now common and understood among clinical workers. However, that does not make it commonly understood by most people outside of the alcoholism/drug addiction treatment field.

The term, **Created Support System Collapse,** is more descriptive of the work you do to put your addict into treatment.

Having said all of that, when you call an alcoholism/drug addiction treatment center to seek assistance, still be prepared to use the term "intervention," because that is the term with which they will be familiar and comfortable.

WHAT TO EXPECT
FROM YOUR COUNSELOR

After you have interviewed several counselors and selected the one to guide and assist you in creating support system collapse, an orderly progression of events will begin to take place.

This counselor will talk with you until he has obtained a very detailed history of your addict's drinking, drugging and behavior. He will also want a detailed history of your relationship with the addict. When he knows enough about your particular situation he will begin to offer advice on selecting the team you are going to put together and suggestions on how to get them to go along with you. Soon after the process begins he will ask for a meeting of the whole team.

At the first group meeting the counselor will probably spend considerable time in getting to know the team members so that he can learn how each fits into the picture. At this and future team meetings, some very interesting facts will likely appear. Some of these facts (about personal relationships) may not be pleasant or easy for you and your fellow team members to deal with. This is where the counselor you have chosen will become so very important. The reason you have carefully selected a person trained to do this work is to help you manage the problems which come up in a Created Support System Collapse.

To help with your study of the disease of addiction, the counselor will either supply you with reading material or give you a list of reading material to obtain on your own. (This book would be helpful to your team members.) Your counselor will probably use films, or lectures with visual presentations, or both to add to your education. You and the others will practice what you're going to say to the addict and how you're going to say it, until everyone is completely prepared to carry through with the part they will play in the process.

In the past when you confronted your addict about his drinking/drugging, nothing changed. Now you are going to enter into a confrontation which is professionally planned, adequately practiced, fully supported, and conducted with unconditional, nonjudgmental love. It will work.

For an idea of what a Created Support System Collapse looks like, take a moment to study the diagram on the next page. ☞

When you see all the arrows pointing towards the ALCOHOLIC/DRUG ADDICT you should **not** feel that anyone is "shooting" at him in an attempt to hurt him. *The idea pictured here is that each person in the circle has something very important to say to him.*

The Created Support System COLLAPSE !

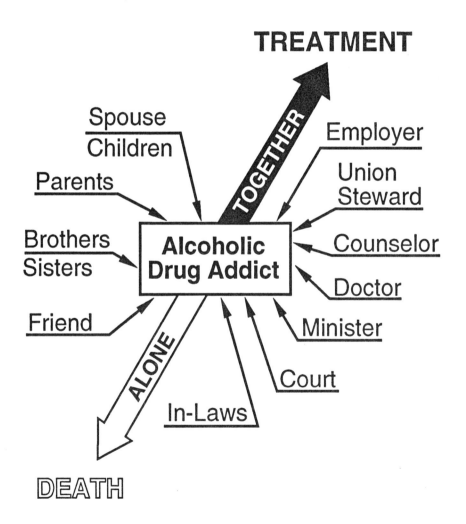

There are other important points being made by the chart. **One:** there are many people (his support system) involved in working to help him. I can't think of a situation where there would be too many people working on the Created Support System Collapse. The reason is that the addict may not be able to *really* hear what is being said to him by one, two, or even three people because he has been scheming and conning people for years. But, he will certainly be impressed by a gathering of a dozen or more people. Simply put, it is very, very difficult to ignore or swindle ten or fifteen people all at once. *(Because no two situations are alike, a large number of people is not a must for every case.)*

Two: there are various levels of relationship and influence represented in the circle. The addict does not always respond to the people you think should be able to reach him. Sometimes it is the person you would think least likely that touches just the right nerve to get the job done. **Three:** Notice the TOGETHER and the ALONE arrows. These indicate the directions the addict can choose to travel for the rest of his life. First the addict is presented with facts, facts, facts and more facts about his drinking and drugging behavior. As the chart shows, these facts are presented to him by his support system (the team members). After he has heard the facts from each of these people who really care about him, he is required to make a choice. He can choose to enter TREATMENT, in which case all of his support system vows to stay *together* with him. The other choice, DEATH, shows that he must go *alone* in that direction, foregoing all support.

If the addict chooses the TOGETHER go to TREATMENT option he can keep his job; keep his spouse; keep his relationship with his children; keep his relationship with his parents; keep his relationship with his brothers and sisters; keep his relationship with his in-laws; and keep all those other relationships which have deep meaning to him. Or, he can refuse to go to treatment and lose everything.

Don't make bets that he will do what you want him to do. Your initial chances of success (getting him into treatment right then) are about 70 to 80 percent. Two or three addicts out of ten will not instantly go to treatment, the day they are confronted by their support system. **However, if the team is well trained and of one mind, it will follow through with leaving these few addicts entirely alone -- without support of any kind.** When this occurs the odds are very great that the addict who at first refuses, will go to treatment reasonably soon after the confrontation.

THIS IS AN EXTREMELY IMPORTANT POINT: THE TEAM WHICH CREATES THE THREAT OF A SUPPORT SYSTEM COLLAPSE MUST BE ENTIRELY READY, WILLING, ABLE AND COMMITTED TO CARRYING THROUGH WITH THE ACTION IT SAYS IT IS GOING TO TAKE. IF THE TEAM DOESN'T CARRY THROUGH WITH ITS ACTION PLAN, THE ADDICT ESCAPES THE CONSEQUENCES OF HIS DRINKING/DRUGGING ONCE AGAIN. HE ESCAPES THE EMOTIONAL PAIN THAT COULD HELP HIM. HIS DENIAL SYSTEM WILL HAVE WORKED VERY WELL. THIS COULD LEAD TO HIS NEVER GOING TO TREATMENT, NEVER RECOVERING.

About ten pages back the word "sabotage" was used. The word sabotage means to undermine, disable, damage, or vandalize something. While it may be difficult for you to understand why anyone would want to destroy the effort to help your addict, you can believe that sabotage occurs all too often. Most of the time the saboteur does not know that he/she is sabotaging the process. Sometimes the saboteurs do what they do deliberately because they feel that they "know what's best" for the addict.

Innocent sabotage occurs when one of the team members appears to be agreeing with all that goes on during the training sessions and then at the crucial time, when the confrontation is about to take place, the innocent saboteur refuses to carry through with his/her role in the process. Or, you have a team member who does not understand the absolute necessity of keeping all discussion of the proceedings within the selected group and word leaks out to the addict. **Deliberate** sabotage occurs when one of the team members goes to the addict and tells him that people are conspiring to take action against him. Or, a team member may deliberately divert the addict away from the confrontation by scheduling an alternate appointment for him at the exact time the team expects to meet with him. The most common sabotage happens *during* the confrontation when one team member, or a sub-group such as the in-laws, becomes charmed by the addict's denial and suddenly joins him in opposition to the team efforts. If that happens you will *really* need the services of the professional you have chosen to lead you. (There are ways to minimize the chances of sabotage happening and if that fails there are ways to deal with it when it does happen. Another reason for the need of a professional guide.)

Okay, sabotage has been prevented or overcome. Your Created Support System Collapse is **WORKING!**

Suddenly your addict says, *"Alright, I'll do whatever you want me to do."*

What happens now?   Most times there is a spontaneous outpouring of love.   After the hugs and kisses you put him in the car and take him to treatment **NOW,** that's what!   You can do it just that quickly because you already have his bags packed, the car warmed up, the treatment center waiting.   Your feeling of relief will be **wonderful.** *Thank your counselor !*

Next you learn about "treatment" and which variety may be best for your addict.

CHAPTER EIGHT

THE RECOVERY JOURNEY BEGINS

(Treatment for the disease of addiction)

It's hard to know where to begin, there are so many forms of treatment. Some are excellent, some are okay, some worthless. Some can even be damaging.

Effective treatment and long-term recovery for alcoholism (and now other drugs), has its beginnings, its seeds, its roots, and its blooming in the 1930s. It all began in Zurich, Switzerland. The seeds that were planted in the early 1930s took root and grew deeply through the mid '30s. The shoots inched upward at the same time. The sprouts broke through into the light of day in 1935 and by 1940 a truly effective treatment for alcoholism was in full bloom. Before 1940 very few people escaped the ravages of the disease of chemical dependency, no matter what drug they used. There were "drying out" places and sanitariums but no *effective* treatment because effective treatment means long-term abstinence from alcohol and/or other drugs.

In 1931 a prominent businessman from New England traveled to Zurich, Switzerland trying to find a way out of his alcoholism. He had gone to Zurich to seek help from the world-renowned psychologist, Carl G. Jung. Following a year of therapy with Dr. Jung, this man returned to the U.S. to resume his business activities. The seeds had been planted. He soon found, however, that even after a year's therapy he could not remain sober. He was once again frequently drunk and unable to function effectively in society.

This man returned to Zurich for more consultation with Dr. Jung and was informed that he must bring about within himself *a profound personality change,* a personality change almost exclusively accomplished with *spiritual means.* If he could not bring about this profound personality change he stood no chance of remaining free of alcohol. The seeds were now beginning to mature, to divide into roots and shoots and move in their ordained direction.

This (once again) dry alcoholic returned to his home area and this time immersed himself in appropriate activities and associations with others who, for reasons of their own (not drug-related) were also attempting to bring about their profound personality change. The sprouts were now breaking through the soil. Because of his efforts and associations, the New England businessman got sober and stayed sober, *free of alcohol*, for the remainder of his life.

In addition to remaining free of alcohol, this alcoholic who had been given the seeds of sobriety by Dr. Jung was able to pass on to a few other alcoholics "the solution" to alcoholism he had received from Dr. Jung. One of the recipients of this solution was able to pass it on to a New York stockbroker in late 1934. The sprouts were now alive in the light of day.

The New York stockbroker got sober and was able to pass along "the solution" to an alcoholic physician from Akron, Ohio. In the early summer of 1935 the sprout had the tiniest of blooms.

Working together for their mutual benefit, this stockbroker and this physician remained alcohol-free for the remainder of their lives. By 1940 the "treatment," whose seeds were planted in the early 1930s, was in full bloom.

The physician lived until 1950; the stockbroker until 1971.

This unlikely pair, this stockbroker and this physician, put together a program for living for themselves and others which makes it possible for alcoholics/drug addicts to bring about within themselves a profound personality change. As a result of this program of profound personality change, addicts can live alcohol/drug free. If you haven't guessed by now, the program these two created is known as **Alcoholics Anonymous.**

It is impossible to calculate the contribution to humanity that was brought about by the sequence of events just described. Because of Alcoholics Anonymous millions of alcoholics, and in recent times those who are addicted to other drugs, have brought about within themselves a profound personality change, gotten sober and stayed sober. Because of Alcoholics Anonymous millions of alcoholics and other addicts have changed from being drains on society to being positive contributors to society.

If the addict you are concerned about is going to attain and maintain sobriety he will have to bring about his own profound personality change. The time-tested, proven method for doing this is to become actively involved in Alcoholics Anonymous or one of the many other addiction recovery programs using the principles of Alcoholics Anonymous (Narcotics Anonymous, Cocaine Anonymous, Drugs Anonymous).

Right about now you may be saying to yourself, "So what, that's not news. I've already heard that Alcoholics Anonymous works. My problem is that my addict won't go to AA or any where else for help."

This book was not written to simply tell you that Alcoholics Anonymous works. It's not that simple.

Indeed if it were that simple you would have no need for **Created Support System Collapse.** All you would need do is say to the addict, "You are sick, go see the doctor." He would go. The doctor would say, "Yes, you are sick. My prescription is for you to go to Alcoholics Anonymous (or NA or CA or DA, etc.)." Your addict would follow the doctor's prescription, get sober and stay sober. You and he would live happily ever after. (Even if your addict went to the doctor when you asked him to go, he wouldn't pay any more attention to him than he pays to you. Right?)

Since you are going to have to use extreme measures to get your addict to seek treatment, which one do you want him to use?

PLACES WHICH PROVIDE TREATMENT FOR ALCOHOLISM/DRUG ADDICTION

You will need some idea of what treatment is all about -- from the standpoint of what they do and how well they do it -- when it is time for you to decide where your addict is going to go to receive treatment. To give you an idea of what each of the various treatment sources does, I will first alphabetically list and describe them. Then I'll discuss each to compare their effectiveness and make recommendations.

TREATMENT PROVIDERS DESCRIBED

ACUPUNCTURIST:

Acupuncture is the Chinese healing art or practice of puncturing the human body in various strategic places with needles. Its purpose is to cure disease or relieve pain.

Acupuncture has been reported as being helpful when used as a companion to other forms of addiction treatment and also as a complete form of treatment. It has been used in both the U.S. and the former Soviet Union.

ADDICTIONIST:

An addictionist is a medical doctor, a physician, who has elected to advance his/her knowledge in the field of addictions treatment; has completed extensive study and been certified for this medical specialty by the American Society of Addiction Medicine. If you want to talk to a medical doctor about someone's drinking/drugging, this is the one.

ALCOHOLICS ANONYMOUS:
(Narcotics Anonymous, Cocaine Anonymous, Drugs Anonymous, etc.)

Alcoholics Anonymous is a self-help program which freely gives its services, and its program to anyone who wants to stop drinking. The book, *Alcoholics Anonymous,* describes in detail its program of recovery. AA is celebrated world-wide as the most successful method of recovery from alcoholism ever known. The AA beginnings are sketched out above.

ALCOHOLISM/DRUG ADDICTION COUNSELOR:

Alcoholism/drug addiction counselors frequently do not have the advanced college educations that other counseling professionals have. However, most A & D counselors are recovering from the disease of alcoholism/drug addiction. Because they are recovering from addiction, they have the advantage of personal experience that counselors with only academic training do not have.

The requirements to become a Certified Addictions Counselor (CAC) vary from state to state, but in general it requires working and studying in a treatment center as an attendant, for two or three years prior to certification. After the required work experience the candidate must demonstrate, to the appropriate state or national governing body, a wide range of counseling expertise. To become certified requires recommendation by supervisors and the passing of extensive written and oral examinations.

While most A & D counselors work only in treatment centers, some do go into private practice. You need to be warned that in some states there is no particular licensing, accreditation, certification, or skill level required before someone decides to go into business for themselves as an A & D counselor.

ALCOHOLISM/DRUG ADDICTION TREATMENT CENTER: (Either free-standing or hospital-based)

Treatment centers are of two general types. Those which are physically located within the confines of a medical or psychiatric acute care hospital are known as hospital-based. Those which offer only addiction treatment and have no connection with an acute care hospital are known as free-standing.

There are some variations of these treatment settings, but it wouldn't help you to go into detail about them here.

Treatment centers generally have to meet the same exacting standards of licensing and accreditation that hospitals have to meet. That is, they will be regulated by their State Division of Mental Health and be required to meet the standards of the national organization, the Joint Commission on Accreditation of Health Organizations. This assures a high level of professional competency.

Most treatment centers utilize what is known as the "multi-disciplinary team approach" to treating the disease of addiction. This means that the center employs a group of treatment professionals who have a wide range of knowledge and skills to provide an all around attack on the disease. This team will probably include medical doctors, (possibly the "addictionist" variety of doctor) psychiatrists, psychologists, social workers, alcoholism/drug addiction counselors, recreational therapists, vocational counselors, marriage and family counselors and others.

AVERSION THERAPY:

Aversion therapy is the use of electricity or drugs to make the person who drinks alcohol suffer sudden pain or extreme sickness. The purpose of aversion therapy is to "condition" the alcoholic to expect that each time he drinks alcohol he will either become violently nauseous and physically sick or experience a terrifying electric shock.

There are also drugs which can be prescribed to narcotic addicts which will block the effects of all narcotics. If the addict uses narcotic drugs while taking the prescribed medication he will not experience any sensation from the narcotic. While this is not aversion therapy, it serves the purpose of telling the addict that there is no point in using narcotics because he can't get "high."

FAMILY PHYSICIAN:

Family physicians are medical generalists, extensively trained to treat and heal a wide variety of human ailments. They are licensed to prescribe drugs, including the psychoactive drugs. Medical schools, however, do a lousy job of teaching physicians how to treat the disease of alcoholism/drug addiction; most don't even try. Medical schools, by and large, only teach physicians how to treat the *complications* of addiction; complications such as liver disease, cardiovascular disease, stomach ulcers, broken bones, etc.

HALFWAY HOUSE:

Halfway houses are temporary homes for recovering alcoholics/addicts, providing them a no-alcohol, no-drug environment until they get used to living without alcohol and/or other drugs. Halfway houses have been around for about 50 years, maybe longer. Residents of halfway houses are required to find a job, work every day, pay for their room and board, abide by the rules of community living and be actively involved in recovering from addiction. The time an addict stays in a halfway house varies from a month to a year or more. Halfway houses are sometimes referred to as "transitional living facilities." State government licensing and certification bodies oversee the activities of halfway houses.

MASTERS of SOCIAL WORK:

MSWs or "social workers" as they are commonly known, are highly educated, skilled counselors. Social workers teach methods of solving emotional/behavioral problems; the problems of everyday living. Social workers tend to specialize in particular fields, depending on their personal interests. You will find them listed in the Yellow Pages of the telephone book under various headings: Social Worker -- Alcoholism -- Drug

Addiction -- Child and Family Counseling -- Marriage and Family Counseling -- Psychotherapy. Some social workers further their education and earn advanced recognition with designations such as "ACSW or "LCSW." LCSW stands for licensed clinical social worker, a designation indicating the highest degree of counseling competence.

METHADONE MAINTENANCE CLINIC:

Methadone is a highly addictive, synthetic narcotic drug. Methadone clinics give, or sell at low cost, the drug methadone to narcotic (and other drug) addicts. The intended purpose is to maintain the addict's drugged condition. Then, supposedly, he will not commit crimes to get the large amounts of money needed to buy drugs from illegal drug dealers. A methadone clinic has to have a building and staff members to operate its program. Buildings and employees cost money. The small amount of money the addicts pay for the drug methadone cannot come anywhere close to providing enough cash to operate such facilities. The people of the U.S., through taxes to the federal government, give the money to pay for these programs.

PSYCHIATRIST:

Psychiatrists are physicians who have elected to specialize in the treatment and healing of people who suffer from mental, emotional and behavioral problems.

Psychiatrists, like other physicians, are licensed to prescribe drugs. Psychiatrists do use psychotherapy but the primary focus of psychiatric medicine is the use of medication (psychoactive drugs) to cure/control mental illness.

PSYCHOLOGIST, CLINICAL:

Psychologists come in several different varieties. Clinical Psychologists specialize in the treatment and healing of people who are suffering from mental, emotional and/or behavioral problems. The work they do is called "psychotherapy" which means they spend a lot of time talking with the patient.

Generally speaking, clinical psychologists are the most extensively trained professionals in the workings of the human mind and human behavior. They are Ph.D. level professionals, licensed to practice the medicine of healing mental/emotional/behavioral conditions. They are not licensed to prescribe drugs, however.

TREATMENT PROCESSES
COMPARED AND RATED

Comparing and rating services which claim to achieve the same results is not easy to do, in a completely unbiased way. So I will tell you right up front that the things I have learned from 27 years of experience in attaining and maintaining sobriety, and 15 years of employment in the field of alcoholism/drug addiction treatment will be reflected in these ratings.

Acupuncture is a method of achieving sobriety that I know nearly nothing about. For all the other sources of help I have extensive, personal, first hand experience as a product user, counselor and treatment program manager.

ACUPUNCTURE:

There are no long-term studies to indicate that acupuncture has any usefulness in the treatment of addiction. I am convinced that almost without exception the only way an alcoholic/drug addict is ever going to get sober and remain continuously sober is through the mechanism of a profound personality change. If this is true, then knowing the nature of acupuncture, it is difficult to understand how it could be of much use in the treatment of addiction. Certainly, acupuncture should *not* be your first line of offense in attacking the disease.

ADDICTIONIST:

There are two "brands" of addictionist; those who are and those who are *not* personally recovering from chemical dependency. Another category, closely related to those who are, is the addictionist who has been motivated to study and treat the disease of addiction because it struck close to him/her in the person of a family member. The difference between these "brands" can best be illustrated by a short story.

Several years ago, following a talk I had given about the disease of alcoholism, I was approached by a Family Practice physician.

"You know," he said, "I can certainly identify with your statement that the care giver's personal experience makes a big difference in the way in which a sick person is given treatment, and the sick person's response to that treatment." He continued, "I learned in medical school that appendicitis was a very painful illness and that the patient needed prompt and competent care to not only relieve the pain but save his life. Therefore, when I had a patient with appendicitis who said, "Oh doctor, it hurts, my God it hurts." I would reply, "Yes, I understand. I am going to do several things to help you right away." "After several years of practicing medicine I was stricken with my own case of appendicitis. Now when a patient tells me that it hurts, I not only understand, I KNOW what they are feeling because I have felt it. That level of knowledge, that level of empathy, is superior to academic understanding.

It makes me a better physician in providing care to someone with appendicitis."

There are competent physicians who work in the field of addiction treatment without the motivation of being an alcoholic/drug addict or having a family member who is addicted. But you need to know that there are differences. Personally, if I'm going to have a garage built, I will hire a carpenter who has built garages.

When you need a physician for an alcoholic/drug addict, find an addictionist. If the addictionist needs other medical specialists to help him, he'll know.

ALCOHOLICS ANONYMOUS:

From it's beginning in 1935 until today, Alcoholics Anonymous has proven to be **THE** way for alcoholics to get and stay sober. Those who have gotten sober and stayed sober through some other form of treatment such as traditional medicine, psychology, religion or voodoo number less than five percent of the total. All the rest got sober and have remained sober because of their activities in Alcoholics Anonymous. It certainly makes sense to go with the program which has, overwhelmingly, the best track record.

In recent years the principles of Alcoholics Anonymous have been copied and put into practice by literally hundreds of other organizations. The most important ones for our consideration are Narcotics Anonymous, Cocaine Anonymous, and Drugs Anonymous. One of these recovery fellowships will prove to be THE way for the alcoholic/drug addict you are concerned with. These are the programs which teach the addict the process of creating one's own profound personality change.

As you can well imagine, a profound personality change doesn't happen quickly. There are no "silver bullets" or magic cures; no shots or surgical procedures to bring about this wonderful happening. Recovery from addiction, whatever the drug, is a lifetime process. If it weren't for Alcoholics Anonymous, only the wealthiest of individuals could afford to pay for a lifetime of professionally sponsored help to achieve a profound personality change. Alcoholics Anonymous and its offspring don't charge anything for their services beyond a request that those who benefit from them pass it on to others who are in need. I know you can readily see the worth and necessity of Alcoholics Anonymous and the rest of the recovery programs based on AA principles.

You should by now also understand that it isn't easy to convince someone they need a profound personality change.

Getting your addict into a life-long recovery program such as Alcoholics Anonymous is easier if he starts with one of the other forms of treatment listed here as a *beginning* point.

ALCOHOLISM/DRUG ADDICTION TREATMENT CENTERS:

Over the past 20 or 25 years alcohol and drug treatment centers have been the beginning point for the majority of people who enter into recovery from the disease of addiction. While it is true that the overwhelming majority of addicts who recover are going to have to become involved with Alcoholics Anonymous or one of its offspring, getting started is very difficult. It is far easier for the addict to begin recovery in the care of a group of professionals, in a setting focused exclusively on recovery. The chances for recovery are much, much better when the addict starts with intensive care.

The best place to get *intensive* care for the disease of addiction is one of the many alcoholism/drug addiction treatment centers now operating in the U.S., and elsewhere around the world.

158

The words "intensive care" were chosen deliberately for this description. Where is a person who is desperately ill, possibly near death, given medical treatment these days? In the local hospital's I C U or Intensive Care Unit, that's where! In an I C U a patient is given direct, hands-on treatment, by a team of several specialists who deal exclusively with the disease that affects that particular patient. Because of the seriousness of their illness they are not simply placed in a general nursing area and looked in on once a day by a physician.

While the average alcoholic/drug addict who is about to enter into a treatment setting is not in immediate physical danger of dying (though some may be), *he is certainly as sick from a terminal illness as anyone who must be admitted to a medical Intensive Care Unit.*

No addict voluntarily enters into an alcohol/drug treatment process. Not one. None ever has and none ever will. If that statement is hard to swallow, please refer back to Chapter Four and study the section on "denial." An addict will forcefully deny that he is sick and needs help. So he doesn't volunteer for this thing. The only thing that *EVER* gets him into treatment is pressure from some source outside himself, something which causes him to have emotional pain. That pressure can be his boss telling him that if he doesn't get his act together he won't have a job. Or, the judge telling him that he has a choice, 30 days in jail or 30 days in a treatment center. Or, when the doctor who is treating his cirrhosis of the liver tells him that he must quit drinking or die. And then says, "Oh, by the way, the best place to stop is the treatment center just down the street. Here's the phone, call them up and make an appointment." Or, the family gets together and interferes with his activities by threatening a "support system collapse." Often it takes all of the above, all of this massive emotional pain, to get the job done.

Think about how sick an alcoholic/drug addict really is. Now think about how much worse he feels because some form of support system collapse has just forced him into treatment. On top of all of this, the only way he knows to deal with pressure -- alcohol or other drugs -- has been taken away from him; he can't get any relief from his feelings. Maybe you now have a little bit of understanding of how difficult it is for an addict to begin recovering from this disease. Do you see why it is so important for the treatment setting to be **intensely** supporting to the addict? I am not asking that you feel sorry for your addict; that might be the worst thing you could do. My request is that you try to understand how difficult this is for him. Such understanding will give you the power to make good decisions.

Because the trauma of going into recovery is so great, the smartest thing you can do for him is to select the best possible setting. **The most protective and intense setting is an inpatient treatment center.** While enrolled in an inpatient treatment center the addict is exposed to a recovery atmosphere twenty-four hours a day, seven days a week, for two or four or more weeks.

In this intense setting, surrounded by others who are starting the recovery process, the addict learns that he is not alone, not unique, in his terrible suffering. He will establish close relationships with others who are recovering from alcoholism/drug addiction and the mutual encouragement to get well that will flow between them cannot be gained, as quickly, in any other setting. **The therapeutic value of this "bonded" relationship between addicts who are beginning the recovery process cannot be overstated.**

Because he remains in treatment for an extended period of time, the multi-disciplinary staff has the opportunity to work with and analyze the addict under varying therapeutic conditions. The staff then has the information it needs to map out a specific plan of "life-changing action" for him. Since the staff is with him around the clock for two to four (sometimes more) weeks, it has the best possible opportunity to help the addict completely agree with and embrace *their* plan for his recovery from addiction.

Of huge importance to the alcoholic/drug addict in an inpatient treatment setting is the fact that he is exposed to Alcoholics Anonymous and Narcotics Anonymous, whether he wants it or not. The majority of alcohol/drug treatment centers provide their patients with an in-depth education about the value of AA/NA/CA and then see that they attend three to six meetings per week while they are in treatment. This familiarity with the self-help recovery programs makes it possible for the addict to be comfortable with attendance at those same meetings after discharge from the primary treatment setting.

There are a great many problems which can, and often do, affect an addict because of the disease of alcoholism/drug addiction. He may need in-depth medical and psychological testing to discover all that is wrong with him. For instance, an addict may be suffering from chronic (not drug related) depression or be manic depressive. He will certainly need specialized treatment for such conditions. He may be suffering from any of 300 to 400 different physical problems brought on by the long-term excessive use of alcohol or other drugs. The medical/psychological diagnosis and care given in alcoholism/drug addiction treatment centers makes them the optimum place to start recovery from addiction and its related ailments.

OUTPATIENT TREATMENT

Many alcoholism/drug addiction treatment centers now offer a form of treatment which is nearly as complete and comprehensive as their residential or inpatient treatment. It is called "outpatient" treatment because the addict/patient does not live in the center around the clock, seven days a week, as he would if he were enrolled in a residential treatment setting. The addict/patient lives at home, continues to work at his job, and attends treatment sessions during evening hours. Attendance in the treatment setting might be three or four hours during the evening, Monday through Friday and four hours on Saturday. The length of treatment varies and may range from eight to 16 weeks, possibly longer.

Outpatient treatment is a lot less intensive than residential treatment because contact with staff members is spread thinly over a longer time and, more importantly, the interaction between patients is reduced from 168 hours a week to maybe 20 hours per week.

Evening outpatient treatment, as just described, works well for the alcoholic/drug addict whose disease has not yet progressed beyond the early part of the crucial phase. A good candidate for evening outpatient treatment would still have his support system (family, job, etc.) solidly in place. A good candidate would be strongly committed to recovery. A good candidate would be able to stop using alcohol and other drugs for an extended period of time -- at least the entire time it takes to complete the course of treatment. If he can refrain from drinking/drugging for that length of time, the recovery process will have an opportunity to take over for him and in him. This freedom from drugs, coupled with his learning to deal with life on life's terms, allows him to overcome the compulsive need to drink or take other drugs.

There are variations of outpatient treatment where the addict/patient attends treatment sessions in a residential setting, with residential patients, during daytime hours and then returns to his home in the evenings. Or, he could reside in a halfway house while undergoing treatment during the day in a residential center. These variations provide a more intense and patient interactive treatment than evening outpatient. They are not, however, as intense as full time residential treatment.

AVERSION THERAPY:

There are not very many aversion therapy treatment centers around, so you are not likely to be confronted with one as a choice. But you might.

Aversion therapy is another name for behavioral conditioning. The hoped-for result is that the alcoholic/addict can be trained to function much like Pavlov's dog. Ring the bell, feed the dog. Ring the bell, feed the dog. Ring the bell, feed the dog. Eventually, when you ring the bell, the dog will slobber and wag his tail whether or not you have any food. Following that line of reasoning, if every time an alcoholic takes a drink he is jolted with electricity or made violently sick, then he will eventually learn that drinking hurts. Then he won't drink anymore. **This presumes that he is able to learn the lesson from the experience. But you have learned, in Chapter Four, that an alcoholic/addict has lost the ability to learn the lesson from the experience when that lesson relates to his drinking and/or drugging.** The lesson most frequently learned by the alcoholics I know (and the lesson I learned) was that if you want to drink, throw away the medication that makes you sick when you drink. As for the electricity, even the most befuddled addict knows not to drink or take drugs while he has his finger stuck in a light socket!

The drug disulfiram, commonly known as Antabuse, is rather widely prescribed by physicians to alcoholics. When someone takes Antabuse and drinks alcohol in any form they become very sick. The experience is one of severe headache, stomach cramps, nausea and vomiting, rapid heart rate and a general feeling of, "Oh, God, I think I'm going to die." Indeed, drinking booze while taking Antabuse has killed people. That certainly solves the problem.

The use of Antabuse for aversion is legitimate when restricted to alcoholics who have a history of *sincerely* trying to follow a treatment program but who are not able to do so. That is, they continue to return to drinking, again and again, even though they are apparently making a genuine effort to get sober. The use of the Antabuse in such cases would be to initially give the alcoholic a few days or weeks free of alcohol. This freedom from alcohol gives him an alcohol-free brain long enough for him to decide whether or not he wants to become completely involved in a recovery program. Use of the Antabuse in this way can be a helpful tool in an overall program of life change. It is not a cure in itself.

If your family doctor, acting alone, wants to use Antabuse as the only form of alcoholism recovery therapy, you should definitely seek a second opinion!

166

HALFWAY HOUSE:

The addict/alcoholic who has worn out his welcome nearly everywhere else and is about to be or already is living on the streets, or the addict whose support system is so screwed up (dysfunctional) as to be counter productive, will find that a halfway house is the ideal place to continue the early phase of recovery from this disease. Most halfway houses require that the addict undergo some form of primary treatment before enrolling in their program. This assures that the addict has been free of alcohol/other drugs for a safe period of time. The reason for this requirement: a halfway house doesn't have a medical staff and cannot afford to take chances on a client/addict being suddenly swamped with a serious medical problem because of withdrawal from alcohol or other drugs.

Halfway houses provide a place to stay, meals and the rules and regulations so necessary to help newly recovering addicts begin the process of becoming responsible for their actions. It is a treatment program that provides wholesome activities, counselors, exposure to recovery principles and most importantly, association with others who are in the early stages of recovery from addiction. Residents of halfway houses are required to get a job and be self supporting.

The cost of living in a halfway house is very reasonable because most of them are non-profit organizations operated by recovering addicts. These are people who are attempting to give back to those in need the thing which was given to them. That "thing" is recovery.

A halfway house provides the best of surroundings to start changing one's personality in profound ways. Addicts who have destroyed their support system are well served by living in a halfway house. Indeed, it may be the only way they stand a chance of getting sober and staying sober.

METHADONE MAINTENANCE CLINICS:

Giving drugs to addicts in an attempt to cure societal problems (crime) was first practiced in England. It was an ill-advised experiment that failed. However, when government bureaucracies get involved with a project, little empires are built. The empire owners will fabricate whatever documentation is necessary to further the existence of their empires. When other governments discover there is a way to spend the people's money "for the good of society," the idea will cross oceans (it gets votes, don't you know). Thus we have in the U.S. the terrible practice of methadone maintenance for narcotic (and other drug) addicts. Methadone is one of the most difficult, if not the most difficult drug to stop using. Addicts who start methadone maintenance become wedded to the clinic that furnishes the drug. They must live close enough to walk to the clinic or, they must drive -- drunk -- to the clinic early *every day* to get their dose of methadone. Then they hang around the clinic neighborhood much of the day drinking booze and doing drugs with the other junkies. Crime is not reduced, it is increased because of methadone maintenance clinics. Methadone is a quick trip to becoming a street zombie.

With few exceptions, legitimate alcoholism/drug addiction treatment centers and addiction therapists avoid working with methadone addicts because their situation is so grave. Your money perpetuates this travesty because the U. S. government subsidizes these clinics.

For the real truth about methadone maintenance clinics as a method of treating the disease of addiction, ask a methadone addict who has finally, and miraculously gotten sober what he thinks about them. One that I know sums it all up this way, "I would (if given the authority) *gladly* burn them all to the ground." This echoes the sentiment of all addicts I know who have broken away from methadone maintenance.

THERAPISTS IN PRIVATE PRACTICE:

There are a half-dozen different professional sources of help for addiction operating in private practice. These are the addictionist, alcoholism/drug addiction counselor, clinical psychologist, family physician, psychiatrist and social worker. (All may also work in a treatment center.)

Ordinarily when you use the services of the private practice professional you will obtain counseling on a one-to-one basis in that professional's office. Typically you will see the counselor (whatever variety) once a week for 50 minutes each visit. The family doctor probably won't give you 50 minutes. There is nothing wrong with that approach to a great many problems. A chemical addiction which has been diagnosed *very* early may respond to such treatment. The advanced case (Crucial or Chronic Phase) **will not** respond to such treatment. The reason for lack of response, if once-a-week, 50 minute counseling is the **only** therapy, is that the alcoholic/drug addict will not stop drinking or taking drugs long enough to become involved in the recovery process that the therapist is trying to promote.

Truly good, ethical, private practice therapists will not attempt to provide treatment to addicts who are frequently using alcohol or other drugs. They will instead insist that the addict be free of the influence of alcohol and other drugs so that effective psychotherapy can take place. Typically they will refer the addict to a more intense, drug-free treatment setting and resume the therapeutic relationship later in the recovery period. Once the addict's brain is free of euphoria-causing chemicals and their residual effects, he can properly benefit from the services of these professionals.

The alcoholic/drug addict whose disease is disturbing people to such an extent that a Created Support System Collapse is being considered has probably gone too far down that snowy hill to benefit from seeing a counselor once a week. *However, each case is different. Your best guide is the professional you have chosen to lead you through a Support System Collapse.*

WHAT TREATMENT IS BEST?

The question arises, "If Alcoholics Anonymous or one of its offspring is going to be the instrument which keeps my addict sober over the long haul, why not bypass those other treatment settings?" "What do we need them for? Let's just go directly to AA." The answer to your question is tied up in the nature of the disease.

Let's assume that you get your addict to go to AA or NA or CA or whatever without first going to some form of primary treatment. A great many do this. However, many, many, many alcoholics/addicts will not hang around AA, NA, CA, etc., long enough for the principles of recovery to take effect.

The AA and AA-type meetings generally last about an hour. With a little fellowship before and after the meeting, the time spent with others who are recovering probably doesn't exceed an hour and 30 minutes. There are meetings all over this planet, 24 hours a day, seven days a week so the opportunity for frequent attendance is available. But the addict who is new to sobriety is not readily convinced that he needs to be free of alcohol and other drugs. His feeling is that all he needs is to be free of trouble.

Because he thinks he only needs to be free of trouble, and after he started attending meetings you got off his back, he doesn't attend meetings often enough. Without **MANY** meetings -- at least one and better yet two or three a day for a year -- he can't get warmly, intimately, consummately, and convincingly involved with the recovery process.

Without the warm, intimate involvement with recovery he gets drunk or stoned because the disease's compulsion takes over. Then he stops going to meetings.

When the binge is over, when his remorse is great and he wants you to get off of his back, he will start going to meetings again. But he won't go to enough of them and he will get drunk again. This can go on for years and years, **if he lives.**

I can tell you from personal experience that this "get sober/then get drunk mess" can last for seven years before true, lasting recovery begins. Others have fought the "sober/drunk/sober" mess for much longer.

Just because there are those who have fought through the "sober/drunk/sober" mess and lived to talk about it, you shouldn't assume that it is a preferred way of achieving lasting sobriety. A huge number of alcoholics and drug addicts have died without making it to continuous sobriety this way.

What treatment is best? The simple answer to the question is, **THE MOST INTENSE, CLOSELY SUPERVISED AND LONG LASTING TREATMENT YOU CAN ARRANGE FOR YOUR ADDICT.**

There are a great many factors to be taken into consideration when you have to make a decision about

173

which treatment setting is best. No two situations are exactly alike. This is one of the areas where you should rely upon the counselor you have chosen to guide you through the process of a Created Support System Collapse. This counselor will have the experience necessary to judge the intensity level best suited for your particular situation..

My recommendation:
INPATIENT TREATMENT -- for two weeks minimum, four or more weeks preferred. If the treatment staff recommends that the addict/patient continue on with primary treatment by living in a halfway house, then you need to make that a condition of your relationship with the addict. If the treatment staff recommends continued primary treatment by having the addict/patient enroll in an outpatient setting, after the inpatient phase, then you need to make that a condition of your relationship with the addict.

If your addict is a physician, religious minister, scientist, attorney or other of great rationalizing power, the treatment recommended may be for three or four months of inpatient treatment. Do not hesitate. Go for it.

The treatment staff will almost certainly recommend that your addict return to the treatment center once or twice a week for an hour or so in the evening to meet with a member of the staff and other addicts who have completed the first phase of primary treatment. These weekly meetings are an extension of the primary treatment program and can continue for a year, maybe longer. This continuation of treatment is called, quite naturally, "continuing care."

The treatment staff may make any of several other recommendations, such as beginning some form of psychotherapy or a continuation of a medical procedure started while the addict was an inpatient.

The treatment staff will absolutely make frequent attendance at meetings of Alcoholics Anonymous, or one of its offspring, NA, CA, DA etc., the number one priority for the recovering alcoholic/drug addict.

Often there are financial considerations which prevent an addict from entering into a private treatment institution. Most large cities (300,000 population) have alcoholism/drug addiction treatment centers which are city or county or state or United Way funded. Much of the time, there will be a waiting period of a few days to three or four weeks before space is available in so called "free" treatment centers. If you plan correctly, utilize the staff of the institution to aid your efforts, and are persistent, you will succeed in getting your addict into the government-funded treatment center.

If financial concerns are bothering you consider this: the cost of three or four weeks of inpatient treatment for alcoholism/drug addiction is about the same as the cost of a good used car. Surely a productive life is worth as much.

If inpatient treatment is not an option, then go with whatever you can get using the advice of the counselor you have chosen to help you — but do something!

THIS IS MOST IMPORTANT!

Use the power you have acquired through the Created Support System Collapse to be absolutely certain that your addict carries through with the plan for recovery the treatment staff creates for him.

Your addict will probably try to change this recovery plan. Don't help him do it.

Don't fall into the trap of thinking that since you know more about your addict than the treatment staff knows, it's okay for you to change his long-range treatment plan. While it may be true that you know more about your addict *personally* than the treatment staff, you certainly don't know more about the disease and the physical/psychological damage that it has caused him.

REMEMBER, IF YOU HAD THE KNOWLEDGE AND ABILITY TO SOLVE THIS PROBLEM YOU WOULD HAVE DONE SO A LONG TIME AGO.

DON'T HELP HIM LEAVE TREATMENT AGAINST STAFF ADVISE.

Your alcoholic/drug addict is in treatment. What do you do now?

You begin to take care of yourself, that's what!

It's going to feel good!

CHAPTER NINE

TIME FOR YOU

(Now you take care of yourself)

In the first chapter I told you there were four terms which would come up again and again; four reasons for writing the book. Those four terms were:
1) **alcohol** and other **drugs**
2) **alcoholism** and **drug addiction**
3) **alcoholics** and **drug addicts**
4) **You**

If you have followed along with me through what I sincerely hope has been an easy, uncomplicated, free-of- technical-jargon description of the first three things, then you know that there is *nothing* you can do about the first two. Alcohol and other drugs are here to stay. They are so deeply imbedded into American and world culture that you nor anyone else can eliminate their usage within the foreseeable future. If alcohol and other drugs are here to stay then the disease of alcoholism/drug addiction is here to stay and it will continue to strike a percentage of those people who use alcohol/drugs just as pneumonia will strike a percentage of people who breathe. There is nothing you nor anyone else can do to prevent alcoholism and/or drug addiction from happening to people who use alcohol/drugs.

There is something, however, that you can do about the third and fourth things.

The third thing: alcoholics/drug addicts are diseased people who respond in a very positive way to a Created Support System Collapse. It is hoped that you will begin the process, or have already begun the process, or have completed the process of doing what you can to bring about recovery from the disease of addiction for your addict. Once you have taken the steps outlined here to create a support system collapse, then it is time for you to do something about the fourth thing -- you.

Once the addict enters treatment he must begin to assume responsibility for himself. If you try to control, or unnecessarily support or direct his activities your actions will sabotage his recovery. Such controlling or unnecessarily supportive actions by you can, and frequently will be, interpreted by him to mean that he doesn't have to become responsible for himself. Such thinking on his part will lead to relapse; a return to drinking and/or drug taking. *You must stop trying to control his actions. You must stop interfering in his life.*

HOW DO YOU DO THAT?

How do you stop doing what you have been doing for so long? You seek help (treatment) for yourself, that's how. Why do you need treatment? Because if you are like the overwhelming majority of people who have interacted with an alcoholic/drug addict for a long period of time your ability to deal with abnormal situations has become warped. *You will have attempted to deal with his abnormal behavior for so long that you will have resorted to your own brand of abnormal behavior just to cope with him.* I know that you do not want to hear this, but it is true. Please check it out with the treatment specialists you are trusting to provide treatment for him.

There are many reasons why your ability to deal with abnormal situations would have become warped over the course of time you have been dealing with your addict. However, that is an entirely different subject from the focus of this book. Check the appendix for good books on this subject.

We really only need to look at one powerful reason why you need help to stop doing what you have been doing for so long. Shame. Guilt. Fault. That's all one reason. Three words, one reason.

If you are the spouse, the child, or the parent of an alcoholic/drug addict then somewhere inside of you is the feeling that if you had behaved differently none of this mess would have happened. You feel shame that someone in your family, someone you love, behaves the way they behave.

You feel guilty because you haven't stopped him from behaving the way he behaves.

It follows then, if you have feelings of guilt and shame about his behavior, his behavior must be your fault. Right? Maybe just a little bit? Since you are a responsible, shame/guilt/fault driven person, you have taken it upon yourself to change your addict, make his behavior acceptable, responsible.

Well I've got news for you! You can't change him! Only he can change him. You've done all that you can possibly do by being the instrument which got him into treatment. Please feel good about yourself for having done that and then begin healing yourself from all that is troubling you, driving you.

WHERE DO YOU FIND TREATMENT FOR YOU?

You find your healing in the fellowships of **AL-ANON** and **NAR-ANON**. Al-Anon and Nar-Anon are recovery fellowships for family members and others who are concerned about, associated with, alcoholics and other drug addicts.

These fellowships are big on **C - C - C.** The **3 Cees** are: Cause - Control - Cure. The message to you is: You didn't *Cause* the disease. You can't *Control* the disease. You can't *Cure* the disease.

The message you need to hear and understand is this. Since you did not Cause the disease there is nothing for you to be ashamed about. Rid yourself of shame. Since you cannot Control the disease there is no reason for you to feel guilty about its going on and on. Rid yourself of guilt. Since you cannot Cure the disease the result of its treatment is not your responsibility. Rid yourself of someone else's responsibility. Nothing here is your fault. Rid yourself of fault. Shame/guilt/fault/responsibility are powerful, deeply entrenched emotional motivations. You cannot simply

183

wish them away, hope them away, want them away and then suddenly be rid of them.

The members of the fellowships of Al-Anon and Nar-Anon are just like you -- suffering from shame/guilt/fault/responsibility. The difference between them and you (if you don't join them) is that they are doing something very constructive with their lives. They have banded together in a mutually supporting effort to rid themselves of shame/guilt/fault/responsibility and many other life-disabling emotions.

The counselor you have chosen to guide you in the Created Support System Collapse will gladly guide you to the nearest meetings of Al-Anon and/or Nar-Anon. This same counselor can also inform you about a variety of inpatient and outpatient treatment programs which could be appropriate to help you with what may well be very rapidly changing conditions in your life.

THE END OF THE BEGINNING

This book has come to an end.
Your work is just beginning.

In the first chapter the idea of taking a journey was presented to you. This was to be a very special journey. A journey out of the prison you shared with your addict. A journey into health, happiness, and peace of mind. By now you should be aware that this special journey, like all things worthwhile, has its price. That price is the pain of perseverance and frustration. Without the pain there is no change.

I sincerely hope that you have committed yourself to this special journey, the journey of action, the journey of change which can put an end to the suffering you have been sharing with your addict.

If you still haven't decided to take the journey, remember . . . .

IF YOU ALWAYS DO WHAT YOU ALWAYS DID, YOU WILL ALWAYS GET WHAT YOU ALWAYS GOT!

APPENDIX

DISEASE CONCEPT

THE DISEASE CONCEPT OF ALCOHOLISM

David L. Ohlm, M. D.

Dr. David Ohlm is a physician and researcher who has devoted a large part of his medical practice to the treatment of alcoholics and drug addicts. Many years ago, in a pioneering spirit, Dr. Ohlm wrote the treatise, THE DISEASE CONCEPT OF ALCOHOLISM. At that time the medical profession acknowledged alcoholism as a disease in name only.

Physicians have only very recently been taught that alcoholism/drug addiction is a diagnosable, treatable disease from which those afflicted can recover.

As recently as 1985 there were only five medical degree universities in the U. S. requiring a core course on alcoholism as a condition for becoming a physician.

If you remember the size of the alcoholism problem from the statistics of Chapter Three, then you have some idea of the significance of the failure of not teaching medical doctors about alcoholism.

It is my belief that the failure to teach soon-to-be physicians about alcoholism is a function of mass stigma. Society, ignorant as it is of the facts, judges alcoholics as shiftless, worthless trash, unworthy of help. Fortunately, there are more medical schools addressing this problem today (1993). When the entire medical profession reaches the conclusion that alcoholism is a disease, society will follow.

I am sincerely grateful to Dr. Ohlm for allowing me to use this piece. Its simplicity, directness and correctness amazed me years ago. It still does.

THE DISEASE CONCEPT OF ALCOHOLISM

There is good news about one of mankind's oldest diseases -- alcoholism. Not too many years ago nearly everybody thought it was hopeless. We don't think so anymore.

The first part of the news is that alcoholism is a true disease, like cancer or high blood pressure. It probably sounds strange to call that "good" news. To show you why it is good, I have to tell you a story.

AA LEADS THE WAY

The story begins in the late 1930's when people who were suffering and dying from alcoholism got tired of going to professionals (physicians, psychiatrists, psychologists) because the professionals couldn't seem to help them -- alcoholics just kept on dying. Or wound up in lunatic asylums or jails. So alcoholics banded together and formed an organization to help themselves -- Alcoholics Anonymous -- and lo and behold, they did discover a way to stop dying and make themselves better.

AA members not only stopped dying and got healthier; they discovered a method that let them give up drinking and lead as normal a life as anyone else. That's the second part of the good news. But in order to help fellow alcoholics, AA first had to decide that alcoholism was a treatable disease. Let's go back to that half of the good news now.

This is my favorite part of the story. Early AA members were all seemingly hopeless drunks who only recently had been able to stop drinking. But the AA program was so successful that finally, after several decades, medical science felt forced to take a good look at it. Why did it work? Why was it that these ordinary people, doing what they did, were able to get well, while we professionals, treating them medically and psychiatrically, seemed to make them sicker rather than better?

The first thing we noticed was that Alcoholics Anonymous people were saying that alcoholism is a primary disease. It is its own disease. It causes its own symptoms -- it is not itself a symptom of some other disease -- and AA treated it this way. And medical science finally had to admit that AA was right. In 1956, the American Medical Association officially recognized alcoholism as a true disease -- an entity of and by itself, that creates its own problems, its own symptoms, that had its own treatment -- and the AMA published this view in a major paper. This turned a lot of things around.

Since 1956 treatment centers have been opened throughout the world where people can go and get decent and humane care for their alcoholism. This has been, believe me, that best possible news.

TRIPPING OVER DEFINITIONS

Now in order to go on with our story, we need to say something about disease. I think we need to define it.

A $.99 pocket dictionary at a book store had something I really liked. It defined disease as anything that interferes with the ability of the human being to function normally. That may be an infection such as tuberculosis which can destroy your lung. Whatever it is, however you caught it, a disease prevents you from living your life as efficiently as you ordinarily would.

And from my point of view, a disease like alcoholism interferes with normal life even more than any other disease because it lasts so long and because the person suffers from it for so many years before anybody really detects the problem and tries to give them help.

But this definition is rather philosophical, and philosophical definitions don't satisfy hard-nosed critics. So we need to go a little further and deal with the concept of alcoholism as a disease -- but from a very scientific, very medical point of view. And if we are going to do that, we need to come up with some definitions of what alcoholism is.

Here's the definition I use and one that I prefer: Alcoholism is a chronic, progressive, incurable disease characterized by loss of control over alcohol and other sedatives.

Now let me explain some of the major words in this much shorter definition. Chronic is self-explanatory. It lasts a long time. The typical adult alcoholic will have 10 or 15 years of sick drinking and lots of secondary problems before he gets help.

Progressive is fascinating. It is one of the unique features of the illness, and one of the reasons why most people in the helping professions -- medicine, counseling, etc. -- do not like alcoholism.

You have to remember that many helping professionals, like many of the rest of us, have at least one alcoholic somewhere in the family. They, just like the rest of us, have that Uncle Jack or Aunt Jane who never got better no matter what anybody did. Poor old Jack. Poor, embarrassing Aunt Jane. The family tried everything it possibly could to help Jack and Jane and that poor wife or husband and those poor kids. An army of experts was brought in -- doctors, psychiatrists, psychologists, social workers, financial advisors, the people who were expert in child-rearing and development -- and none of it helped because Jack and

194

Jane (who did not deserve much sympathy after awhile) went right on drinking. That is part of the meaning of progressive -- it goes on and on and on. And it demoralizes everyone involved. It tends to make them say,"What's the use?" -- almost from the beginning.

ALCOHOLISM DOES NOT GO AWAY

The other part of progressiveness that fascinates me is that, as the alcoholic continues to drink, the disease can only get worse, progressively worse. But let's say that Jack or Jane stops drinking. Maybe because of some formal treatment or maybe he or she just goes on the wagon, and there is a prolonged period of sobriety for, say, 10 or 15 or even 25 years. Then for some reason, usually very trivial, Jack or Jane decides they can drink again and tries to return to normal, social, controlled type of drinking that any non-alcoholic can get away with. But poor Jack or Jane cannot get away with it.

Within a short period of time, usually within 30 days, the symptoms that the alcoholic will show are the same symptoms shown when drinking was stopped 25 years before. And usually worse. It is almost as if the alcoholic had not had that 25 years of sobriety, as if they meant nothing. An alcoholic cannot stay sober for awhile and start over and have early symptoms of alcoholism. An alcoholic cannot enjoy a few years of good drinking before it gets as bad as it was before. It is right there waiting and takes up where it left off. I know this is shocking -- it has a hint almost of the supernatural. Later I think I can give you a scientific explanation as to why it is a medical fact.

IN PURSUIT OF DEFINITION

But let's go on with the definition. Alcoholism is an incurable disease -- that to me is undeniable. Uncle Jack or Aunt Jane can return to normal life, but only for as long as drinking is stopped. You will come upon an occasional, rare medical study that says differently -- that says an alcoholic can be taught to handle controlled social drinking. If you are an alcoholic, do not believe it. Science has so far given us no cure for alcoholism.

Now, we have said that alcoholism is a chronic, progressive, incurable disease characterized by loss of control over alcohol and other sedatives. It is characterized by loss of control. That may sound so obvious as to be trivial, but it is a very important medical definition. It is what makes this disease different from other chronic, incurable disease such as diabetes and arthritis of some types. Loss of control does not mean, as many layman and indeed professionals seem to think, that when an alcoholic takes a drink -- every time he takes a drink -- he is going to drink to excess and get drunk.

That is very rare. Most of my patients tell me that there were times right before they landed in the hospital when they had a drink or two on a given occasion--and then stopped. They had no more alcohol that day. And if you would look at that little 24 hour period, you would assume that such people were normal, controlled drinkers. But what loss of control means is that once the alcoholic takes that first drink after a period of being sober or abstinent, he cannot predict with any reliability whether he is going to have a normal or abnormal drinking episode.

ALCOHOLISM-SEDATIVISM

Now this is probably a good place to tell you that alcohol is a sedative and to point out the implications of that fact. Alcoholism is a chronic, progressive, incurable disease characterized by loss of control over alcohol and other sedatives. The alcoholic has lost control over not just the drug alcohol -- for alcohol is basically nothing more than a widely available, socially acceptable, non-prescription and inexpensive tranquilizer or sedative. It is one that you can go buy in the liquor store or supermarket rather than a pharmacy. But if you look at it as a drug -- if you look at what it does to the brain -- it is a sedative. It works by putting brain tissue to sleep just like a tranquilizer or sleeping pill.

You can probably see that we have got a trick issue here. Because if the alcoholic has lost control over alcohol, that is not the only drug he has lost control over; he has lost control over all other sedative drugs as well. And indeed, one of the really big problems in current treatment, at least among the patients I see, is that the majority (60%) are not only abusing ethyl alcohol, they are also abusing minor tranquilizers and sleeping pills -- sedative drugs that, interestingly enough, they usually get by prescription legally from physicians who: A) do not know that they are treating alcoholics or B) do not know how to treat alcoholism and do not recognize alcoholism as a disease that is characterized also by loss of control over the very drugs that they are prescribing.

So you can rapidly end up with someone who is not only addicted to ethyl alcohol but also hooked on tranquilizers and sleeping pills, and he will probably switch back and forth from one to the other.

We now know what alcoholism is: a chronic, progressive, incurable disease characterized by loss of control over alcohol and other sedatives. This is the definition I like to use clinically. If I have a patient sitting in my office, and I am trying to make the decision, "Does Jack or Jane have alcoholism?", this is the definition I go to work with. Loss of control is the most important clinical factor. Does this individual have predictable behavior when he drinks? If he does, then he is not an alcoholic. But if his behavior is not predictable when he drinks -- if he simply cannot tell what will happen next -- then I know the disease has got him.

HOW MEDICINE DEFINES "DISEASE"

Though doctors like to talk about a disease's cause or etiology, necessity compels us to look first at signs and symptoms. Signs are the physical marks a doctor can literally see in a sick individual -- for example, the fever that accompanies pneumonia or the sugar that a diabetic will have in his urine. Are there unique symptoms for the mysterious disease we call alcoholism?

Absolutely. There are probably more than for most diseases, and we know a good deal about them.

I will not go through all the signs and symptoms -- there are 50 or 60 common ones and many others not so common -- but I do want to mention a few that might be called highlights. In the early stages, for instance, you have what is known as relief drinking. An individual uses alcohol to get relief from something: physical pain, money worries -- it could be anything. Drunk driving commonly occurs in the early stages of alcoholism. Also memory blackouts. That is a period of amnesia that occurs while the person is drinking.

If you know an individual who has had that experience more than once or twice, the odds are that this person is an alcoholic. Relief drinking, drunk driving, blackouts -- these are all early stage symptoms.

Then we get to the middle stage of the disease. This is commonly called the crucial stage because it is here that most alcoholics can be detected and gotten into treatment. It is also the period when, if you do not get them into treatment, the chances for recovery go down; so it is in fact extremely crucial.

It is in this stage that we see the classic symptoms: absenteeism from work, poor job performance, financial problems, family problems, the changes in moral or ethical behavior that tend to occur as the disease gets worse (and help the alcoholic to be disliked). These are the signs and symptoms that make the disease fairly visible and detectable -- it could be the lucky time if the afflicted person somehow starts to get some treatment.

And treatment is certainly needed because this is the beginning of alcoholism's physical problems as well.

Once the deterioration of the body starts, the alcoholic has entered the late or chronic stages of the disease.

Most of us, when we think of an alcoholic, picture the chronic-stage person. The semi-human down there with the body gone rotten, the liver shot, the brain only flickering a little and about to go out. Generally, we picture the skid row bum who -- in fact -- makes up 3%, maybe 4%, of the alcoholics in the world. Most alcoholics are not fortunate enough to live to reach that stage. Most alcoholics will die traumatically -- on a highway or at home with a cigarette that they forgot to put out and it burns up their bed with them in it.

LIFE-SAVING VALUE
OF DISEASE CONCEPT

All right. We have now become very gloomy -- which is the natural pathogenesis of alcoholism when it goes its way without treatment. But the wonderful thing about disease concept is that it allows us to detect the alcoholic's symptoms and get him into proper treatment before the damage is irreversible. And once in the proper treatment, complete and total recovery is highly probable.

In the United States today roughly 34.5 out of every 36 people who have alcoholism are going to die from it, one way or another. It is going to kill them. And they will never have been treated for it.

Alcoholics get all kinds of labels stuck on them. And a lot of treatment -- frequently with other sedative drugs which drive the addiction in even more deeply and shove the alcoholic downhill even faster. Treatment is available, but it is often simply the wrong treatment. Therefore, naturally ... the alcoholic dies.

The luckier ones die. About half of 1% of every 36 will go insane. They will wind up with physical brain damage or "Wet Brain" which you have probably heard about. So much of the brain tissue is destroyed in these late stages of alcoholism that the only thing to be done with the alcoholic is to put him in a state hospital or nursing home.

So a significant number of alcoholics will eventually have their minds destroyed by the disease. About 34 out of 36 will be killed by it in one way or another. One out of 36 will get treatment, will recover and get well. That is a tragic statistic. It is tragic because it is

202

unnecessary. For we do have the proper treatment now -- the treatment of alcoholism as a primary disease -- and with proper treatment these awful numbers are changed completely around.

Look at these statistics. Let's say that we have caught someone in the throes of middle-stage alcoholism. The classic case is someone who is still employed but has been forced into treatment by an employer because of deteriorating job performance. In this situation, recovery rates are as high as 80%. Eight out of 10 middle-stage alcoholics can get well! We cannot expect the same for late or chronic-stage alcoholics; but even there -- among skid row types, the worse cases you can think of -- the recovery rates run from 25% to 30% to 35%. By "recovery," I mean people regaining their health and going back to normal, functioning, working lives. This is another strange aspect of the disease we call alcoholism. There are very few chronic, progressive, incurable illnesses where 25% to 80% of those who have them can get well.

ALCOHOLISM -- THE CAUSE

What causes alcoholism? We do not know for sure, but we now have some pretty good ideas. Medical research has shown, for example, that alcoholism runs in families. (You probably have noticed that tendency from your own observation.) Family history taken from patients indicate that, 95% of the time, the mother had a drinking problem or the father did or an uncle or brother. Usually when there is one alcoholic in a family, you will find many more in the background. Nor is this largely a matter of environment. Heredity studies done all over the world clearly show that genetics is far more significant in determining whether or not you will be an alcoholic than any other single factor examined. Genetics is more significant than any combination of social or environmental factors examined.

Now I am not saying a person is born an alcoholic. No. I have never met an alcoholic who did not drink. But I think it is conclusive that some people are predisposed to alcoholism because of their heredity; and if they ever start drinking, they run an unbelievably high risk of developing the disease.

THIQ – BIOCHEMICAL CULPRIT

Of course, in medicine we have a lot of diseases that work that way. Diabetes has a high family predisposition. So, probably, does heart disease. Now, when medical science notices a family predisposition toward a disease, it will look for some abnormality in body chemistry. What about the body chemistry of alcoholics?

It started down in Houston, Texas with a medical scientist named Virginia Davis who was doing cancer research. For her studies she needed fresh human brain -- which is not widely available; you do not run down to the store and buy it. So she would ride out with the Houston police in the early morning, and they would pass along skid row and collect the bodies of the winos who died overnight. She removed the brains for her cancer research.

Virginia discovered in the brains of those chronic alcoholics a substance that is, in fact, closely related to heroin. This substance, long known to scientists, is called Tetrahydroisoquinoline -- or (fortunately) THIQ for short. When a person shoots heroin into his body, some of it breaks down and turns into this THIQ. But then these people had not been using heroin; they had just been simple alcoholics. So how did the THIQ get there?

When the normal adult drinker takes in alcohol, it is very rapidly eliminated at the rate of about one drink per hour. The body first converts the alcohol into something called acetaldehyde. This is very toxic stuff, but Mother Nature helps us get rid of acetaldehyde very quickly by changing it into carbon dioxide and water which is eliminated through our kidneys and lungs.

What Virginia discovered in Houston, what has been extensively confirmed since, is that something additional happens in the alcoholic. In them, a very small amount of poisonous acetaldehyde is not eliminated; instead, it goes to the brain where, through a very complicated biochemical process, it winds up as this THIQ I mentioned before. Researchers have found out fascinating things about THIQ.

First, THIQ is manufactured right in the brain, and it only occurs in the brain of alcoholic drinkers. It does not happen in the brain of the normal social drinker of alcohol.

Second, THIQ has been found to be much more addicting than morphine.

The third fascinating item about THIQ also has to do with addiction. There are, as you might know, certain kinds of rats that cannot be made to drink alcohol. Put them in a cage with a very weak solution of vodka and water, and they will refuse to touch it. They will literally thirst to death before they agree to drink alcohol. But if you take the same kind of rat and put an unbelievably minute quantity of THIQ into the rats brain--one quick injection--the animal will immediately develop a preference for alcohol over water. It will scurry across the cage to get to that vodka and water. In fact, he will be happier if you mix his drink with less and less water. So we have taken a teetotaling rat and turned him into an alcoholic rat. And all we needed was a smidgin of THIQ.

Other studies have been done with monkeys, our close animal relatives in medical terms. We have learned that once THIQ is injected into a monkey's brain, it stays there. You can keep a THIQed monkey dry, off alcohol, for as long as 7 years; then when you sacrifice him and study his brain, that weird stuff is still there. This, as you have probably already seen, takes us back to the progressiveness of the disease. Remember that person who has been sober for 10 or 25 years and then suddenly started drinking again? The alcoholic will immediately show the same symptoms displayed years before -- and it is no wonder! The human alcoholic is still carrying THIQ like those man-made alcoholic monkeys and rats.

THE PIECES BEGIN TO FIT

You see how beautifully these laboratory findings fit in with what we specialists in alcoholism have long noticed in our clinics. Uncle Jack is brought in, and he is drunk again; and even though it is slowly killing him, he somehow cannot stop drinking. When he is sober enough we will get a family history. Yes, there are other alcoholics in his family; there is a family predisposition -- an abnormality in the family body chemistry -- which we only saw the shadow of before. But now we see it much more clearly: it is a predisposition toward making THIQ.

Now alcoholics do not intend to make THIQ when they start drinking. They do not mean for their brains to manufacture something stronger than morphine -- they have been warned about the evils of narcotics all their lives. But they have heard a good deal less about the evils of alcoholism. Most normal Americans take a drink now and then, and the young alcoholics-to-be want to be normal. So they take a drink now and then, too. Unfortunately, the alcoholics-to-be are not normal. They do not know about the predisposition toward THIQ-making their brain chemistry has inherited. Nobody knew about it until fairly recently. So Jack and Jane and a new generation have their first few drinks, and everything seems cool.

So the alcoholic-to-be starts drinking, and he or she may well be very moderate at first. Just a few on Saturday nights. Maybe a nip or two to calm down while fixing dinner for the family. Two or three drinks to quiet the jitters before high school graduation. In the beginning, the alcoholics-to-be only get seriously drunk say, once or twice a year. So far, so good. But all this time the alcoholic brain is humming away in there building its little cache of THIQ, just like the brains of our rats and monkeys. At some point, maybe sooner, maybe later, the alcoholic will pass over a shadowy line into a whole new way of life.

Now medical science still does not know where this line is -- does not know how much THIQ an individual brain will pile up before the big event happens. Some predisposed people cross the line while they are teenagers -- or earlier! It will not occur in others until they are 30 or 40, maybe even retired. But once it does happen, the alcoholic will be as hooked on alcohol as he would have been hooked on heroin if he had been shooting that instead -- and for very similar chemical reasons! Now comes loss of control. Now its chronic, progressive, incurable nature is obvious to practically everyone who knows the alcoholic. Now it is all too clearly a disease. And now, all too often -- it is a disease that will mainly get treated with other sedatives. Far too often, alcohol addiction is treated with pills that keep the disease raging. When we are done, if the alcoholic is still alive, he will be about as functional as a THIQed rat.

GOOD NEWS

Alcoholism is a disease -- and that is good news. Alcoholism is not the alcoholic's fault -- and that is good news too. Alcoholics can today get proper treatment for the disease, and that treatment begins when we tell them these facts. The alcoholic patients I see are usually hugely relieved to hear that it is not their fault because they have been carrying tons of guilt along with the alcoholism.

Now, instead of guilt, the alcoholic person can take on some responsibility. Now that the alcoholic knows the facts, he or she can, with treatment, take the responsibility of stopping the drinking; alcoholics can refuse to put more THIQ into their brains; and they can, with treatment, be taught how to control it.

Alcoholics can learn how to live like normal grown-ups again. That is good news for all of us.

BOOKS YOU MIGHT WANT TO READ AS YOU TRAVEL THE ROAD OF RECOVERY

There are hundreds of books on the subject of addiction to alcohol, and other drugs. The following list is not intended to cover everything available on the subject. As you start someone on their journey, and begin your own, you will discover the right reading path for you. These are only suggested as a beginning point.

Most communities have several sources of information on alcoholism/drug addiction. Check your local library under the heading *alcoholism*. Check the Yellow Pages of your telephone book under the headings of addiction, alcoholism, and drug addiction, and you will find organizations which sell these books. Many bookstores now have a specific section devoted to "recovery books" or self-help/psychology.

Alcoholics Anonymous
This is THE text for recovery from alcoholism.
   Order from:
Alcoholics Anonymous
P. O. Box 459 Grand Central Station
New York, NY 10017
Phone: (212) 686-1100

Narcotics Anonymous
This is NA's text. NA is an outgrowth of AA for those who identify more with pills, needles, snorting, and smoking dope than they do with drinking alcohol.
   Order from:
Narcotics Anonymous
World Service Office
P. O. Box 9999
Van Nuys, CA 91409
Phone: (818) 780-3951

Al-Anon Family Groups
This text describes the purpose and workings of Al-Anon, an organization devoted to supporting those who have a relationship with an alcoholic. For teenagers and youngsters as well as adults
   Order from:
Al-Anon Family Group Headquarters, Inc.
P. O. Box 862 Midtown Station
New York, NY 10018-0862   Phone: (212) 302-7240

Nar-Anon Family Groups Newsletter
Nar-Anon is an organization supporting those who have a relationship with a drug addict.
Order from:
Nar-Anon Family Groups
P. O. Box 2562
Palos Verdes, CA 90274
Phone: (213) 547-5800

Bear Facts
A newsletter published by Co-Dependents Anonymous. CoDA is a self-help organization supporting those who grew up in homes with big-time relationship problems, and/or those who want to improve upon their current relationships.
Contact:
Co-Dependents Anonymous
P. O. Box 33577
Phoenix, AZ 85067-3577
Phone: (602) 277-7991

Intervention
By Dr. Vernon E. Johnson
Dr. Johnson pioneered the process of creating a support system collapse to coerce alcoholics/drug addicts into treatment, called it "intervention," and wrote about it in his book, *I'll Quit Tomorrow.* The book *Intervention,* elaborates on that process.

Order from:
The Johnson Institute
510 First Avenue North
Minneapolis, MN 55403-1607
Phone: (800) 231-5165
In Minnesota (800) 247-0484

Codependent No More
(How to Stop Controlling Others and Start Caring for Yourself)
By Melody Beattie
If you have been intimately associated with an alcoholic/drug addict for a considerable length of time, you could (and probably should) be labeled as "codependent." If so, this and dozens of other titles by other great authors, could bring serenity and peace-of-mind to your life.
Order from:
Hazelden Educational Materials
P. O. Box 176
Center City, MN 55012-0176
Phone: (800) 328-9000
In Minnesota (800) 257-4010

The Recovery Resource Book
By Barbara Yoder
An 8 1/2" x 11", 314 page collection of information on the addictive disorders. It covers alcohol, nicotine, street drugs, prescription drugs, food, love, work,

codependence, gambling, sex, debt, and money. Most of the known "self help" organizations are listed with addresses and telephone numbers. Dozens and dozens of books are reviewed with information given on where to buy them. If you're searching for information on addiction, this is the place to start. The technical/scientific/academic world of research/speculation on the subject is not covered. But don't worry about that. Such information is useless for the task you have before you.

Order from:
Fireside Books
Simon & Schuster Building
Rockefeller Center
1230 Avenue of the Americas
New York, NY 10020

The Natural History of Alcoholism
By George E. Vaillant, M.D.
This is a highly regarded, extensively researched, scientific/technical/academic treatise on alcoholism. Written by a psychiatrist, it covers all sides of alcoholism from a scientific outlook. This is not comfortable, easy, fireside reading. Check it out at the library before deciding to buy.

Published by:
Harvard University Press, Cambridge, MA

INDEX

INDEX

ORDER YOUR PEACE OF MIND TODAY

If you've found this book in a waiting room it's here for everyone who comes in. Please don't take the book away from this area. To get your personal copy of the book, cut or tear one of the forms from the next pages and order today.

Ordering is easy. You may call us at the phone number given and use your credit card. Or FAX the information, using your credit card. Or order by mail with check, money order or credit card. Most orders are shipped the day they are received; all within 24 hours.

As a special offer, postage paid shipping (at book rate) will be included in the cost of the book if you order from this form. NOTE! The U. S. Postal Service can take 3 to 4 weeks to deliver at book rate. For 2 or 3 day delivery, include 1st Class postage.

If someone's drinking and/or drug taking worries you, this book is must reading. You can do something positive about it. You can put a stop to their drinking/drugging and your worrying. It's all explained here.

If you are using the last order form, please tell us the name and address where you found the book. Thanks.

TO ORDER THIS BOOK
YOU MAY REMOVE THIS PAGE

**Fill in information on the other side then
Mail, Phone, or FAX
to:**

ABYSS PUBLISHING
**Mailstop 350
11831 Kingston Pike
Knoxville, TN 37922**

PHONE (615) 694-5055

FAX (615) 675-0871

TO ORDER
REMOVE THIS PAGE
Fill in the information on the other side

ORDER FORM
Mail, Phone, or FAX
Address on the Back of this Page

Please send me the book:
End Their Drinking?   Drug Taking?
YOU DECIDE

Name:_____

Please Print

Address:_____

City:_____

State:_____Zip_____

Book cost: postage paid . . . . $ 17.95
1st Class Postage: $2.90 . . . . $.
Tenn. residents add $1.48 Sales Tax . . . . . $.
Total enclosed . . . . $.

(Without 1st class postage book may take 3 to 4 weeks to arrive)

Payment by: ( )Check   ( )Money order
                 ( )Visa   ( )Master Card

Card number: _____

Name on card: _____

Expiration date:_____

TO ORDER THIS BOOK
YOU MAY REMOVE THIS PAGE

**Fill in information on the other side then
Mail, Phone, or FAX
to:**

ABYSS PUBLISHING
Mailstop 350
11831 Kingston Pike
Knoxville, TN 37922

PHONE (615) 694-5055

FAX (615) 675-0871

TO ORDER
REMOVE THIS PAGE
Fill in the information on the other side

ORDER FORM
Mail, Phone, or FAX
Address on the Back of this Page

Please send me the book:
End Their Drinking?   Drug Taking?
YOU DECIDE

Name:_____
Please Print
Address:_____

City:_____

State:_____Zip_____

Book cost: postage paid . . . . $ 17.95
1st Class Postage: $2.90 . . . . $.
Tenn. residents add $1.48 Sales Tax . . . . . $.
Total enclosed . . . . $.

(Without 1st class postage book may take 3 to 4 weeks to arrive)

Payment by: ( )Check   ( )Money order
                   ( )Visa   ( )Master Card

Card number: _____

Name on card: _____

Expiration date:_____

TO ORDER THIS BOOK
YOU MAY REMOVE THIS PAGE

**Fill in information on the other side then
Mail, Phone, or FAX
to:**

**ABYSS PUBLISHING
Mailstop 350
11831 Kingston Pike
Knoxville, TN 37922**

PHONE (615) 694-5055

FAX (615) 675-0871

**TO ORDER
REMOVE THIS PAGE
Fill in the information on the other side**

ORDER FORM
Mail, Phone, or FAX
Address on the Back of this Page

Please send me the book:
End Their Drinking?   Drug Taking?
YOU DECIDE

Name:_____
Please Print
Address:_____

City:_____

State:_____Zip_____

Book cost: postage paid . . . . $ 17.95
1st Class Postage: $2.90 . . . . $.
Tenn. residents add $1.48 Sales Tax . . . . . $.
Total enclosed . . . . $.

(Without 1st class postage book may take 3 to 4 weeks to arrive)

Payment by: ( )Check   ( )Money order
                          ( )Visa   ( )Master Card

Card number: _____

Name on card: _____

Expiration date:_____

TO ORDER THIS BOOK
YOU MAY REMOVE THIS PAGE

Fill in information on the other side then
Mail, Phone, or FAX
to:

ABYSS PUBLISHING
Mailstop 350
11831 Kingston Pike
Knoxville, TN 37922

PHONE (615) 694-5055

FAX (615) 675-0871

TO ORDER
REMOVE THIS PAGE
Fill in the information on the other side

ORDER FORM
Mail, Phone, or FAX
Address on the Back of this Page

Please send me the book:
End Their Drinking?   Drug Taking?
YOU DECIDE

Name:_____

Address:_____

City:_____

State:_____Zip_____

Book cost: postage paid . . . . $ 17.95
1st Class Postage: $2.90 . . . . $.
Tenn. residents add $1.48 Sales Tax . . . . . $.
Total enclosed . . . . $.

(Without 1st class postage book may take 3 to 4 weeks to arrive)

Payment by: ( )Check   ( )Money order
                   ( )Visa   ( )Master Card

Card number: _____

Name on card: _____

Expiration date:_____

TO ORDER THIS BOOK
YOU MAY REMOVE THIS PAGE

**Fill in information on the other side then
Mail, Phone, or FAX
to:**

ABYSS PUBLISHING
Mailstop 350
11831 Kingston Pike
Knoxville, TN 37922

PHONE (615) 694-5055

FAX (615) 675-0871

TO ORDER
REMOVE THIS PAGE
Fill in the information on the other side

ORDER FORM
Mail, Phone, or FAX
Address on the Back of this Page

Please send me the book:
End Their Drinking?   Drug Taking?
YOU DECIDE

Name:_____
Please Print

Address:_____

City:_____

State:_____Zip_____

Book cost: postage paid . . . . $ 17.95
1st Class Postage: $2.90 . . . . $.
Tenn. residents add $1.48 Sales Tax . . . . . $.
Total enclosed . . . . $.

(Without 1st class postage book may take 3 to 4 weeks to arrive)

Payment by: ( )Check   ( )Money order
                 ( )Visa   ( )Master Card

Card number: _____

Name on card: _____

Expiration date:_____

TO ORDER THIS BOOK
YOU MAY REMOVE THIS PAGE

**Fill in information on the other side then
Mail, Phone, or FAX
to:**

ABYSS PUBLISHING
**Mailstop 350
11831 Kingston Pike
Knoxville, TN 37922**

PHONE (615) 694-5055

FAX (615) 675-0871

TO ORDER
REMOVE THIS PAGE
Fill in the information on the other side

ORDER FORM
Mail, Phone, or FAX
Address on the Back of this Page

Please send me the book:
End Their Drinking?   Drug Taking?
YOU DECIDE

Name:_____
Please Print
Address:_____

City:_____

State:_____ Zip_____

Book cost: postage paid . . . . $ 17.95
1st Class Postage: $2.90 . . . . $.
Tenn. residents add $1.48 Sales Tax . . . . . $
Total enclosed . . . . $.

(Without 1st class postage book may take 3 to 4 weeks to arrive)

Payment by: ( )Check   ( )Money order
                  ( )Visa   ( )Master Card

Card number: _____

Name on card: _____

Expiration date:_____

TO ORDER THIS BOOK
YOU MAY REMOVE THIS PAGE

**Fill in information on the other side then
Mail, Phone, or FAX
to:**

**ABYSS PUBLISHING
Mailstop 350
11831 Kingston Pike
Knoxville, TN 37922**

PHONE (615) 694-5055

FAX (615) 675-0871

TO ORDER
REMOVE THIS PAGE
Fill in the information on the other side

ORDER FORM
Mail, Phone, or FAX
Address on the Back of this Page

Please send me the book:
End Their Drinking?   Drug Taking?
YOU DECIDE

Name:_____
                    Please Print
Address:_____

City:_____

State:_____Zip_____

Book cost: postage paid . . . . $ 17.95
1st Class Postage: $2.90 . . . . $.
Tenn. residents add $1.48 Sales Tax . . . . . $.
Total enclosed . . . . $.

(Without 1st class postage book may take 3 to 4 weeks to arrive)

Payment by: ( )Check   ( )Money order
                 ( )Visa   ( )Master Card

Card number: _____

Name on card: _____

Expiration date:_____